Lektürehilfen

Willy Russell

Educating Rita

von Margaret von Ziegésar
und Detlef von Ziegésar

Klett Lernen und Wissen

Margaret von Ziegésar, gebürtige Engländerin, Englischlehrerin und Schulbuchautorin.
Dr. Detlef von Ziegésar, Professor em. für englische Sprache und Kultur und deren Didaktik an der Pädagogischen Hochschule Karlsruhe.

Die Seiten- und Zeilenangaben der Lektürehilfe beziehen sich auf die Textausgabe: Willy Russell, Educating Rita, hrsg. von Bernhard Reitz, Stuttgart: Reclam, 1997 (Universal-Bibliothek Nr. 9040; Fremdsprachentexte).

Bibliographische Information Der Deutschen Bibliothek
Die Deutsche Bibliothek verzeichnet diese Publikation in der Deutschen Nationalbibliographie; detaillierte bibliographische Daten sind im Internet über http://dnb.ddb.de abrufbar

Auflage 4. 3. 2. 1. | 2009 2008 2007 2006
Die letzten Zahlen bezeichnen jeweils die Auflage und das Jahr des Druckes.

Dieses Werk folgt der reformierten Rechtschreibung und Zeichensetzung. Ausnahmen bilden Texte, bei denen künstlerische, philologische oder lizenzrechtliche Gründe einer Änderung entgegenstehen.

Internetadresse: http://www.klett.de
Umschlagfoto: dpa Picture-Alliance GmbH, Frankfurt/M.
Satz: DTP Andrea Eckhardt, Neuhausen
Druck: CPI books, 25912 Leck
Printed in Germany
ISBN-13: 978-3-12-923028-2
ISBN-10: 3-12-923028-9

9 783129 230282

Contents

The Author and His Times

Educating Rita is to a large degree autobiographical. Like Rita, William Martin Russell, born in 1947, was also brought up in a working class family. They lived on a housing estate just outside Liverpool. His father worked in a factory before buying a fish-and-chip shop and his mother had a job in a warehouse. His experience of school is mirrored in Rita's description on p. 31. He, too, shared his schoolmates' antipathy towards education and once described his school days in an interview:

> "When I was eleven they sent me to a secondary school in Huyton. Like all the other Knowsley kids I was frightened of Huyton. There were millions of new houses there and flats, and everyone said there were gangs with bike chains and broken bottles and truck spanners. What everyone said was right; playtime had nothing to do with play, it was about survival. Thugs roamed the concrete and casually destroyed anything that couldn't move fast enough. Dinner time was the same only four times as long. If you were lucky enough to survive the food itself then you had to get out into the playground world of protection rackets, tobacco hustlers, trainee contract killers and plain no-nonsense sadists. And that's without the teachers!" (Glaap, 1984, pp. 88–90)

Consequently, when Russell left school at 15 he only had one O-level, in English, and the vague idea of becoming a writer. However, with his social background he had no idea how to go about it. So he worked as a ladies' hairdresser until he was 20. Although he regarded art as alien to his world, he did become interested in the Liverpool Beat Poets (among them the Roger McGough mentioned by Rita in Act I, scene 1) and in folk-music. He played the guitar in pubs and wrote some songs.
Russell describes his initial distaste for plays and the theatre as follows, "Theatre had always seemed to me a highbrow slap in the face to people like me. I just couldn't relate to it, either culturally or socially; it didn't seem to me to be about people like me, and people like me never seemed to go and look at it" (*The Independent*, 23. 1. 88). In another interview he expanded on this view:

> "They are bourgeois plays because they are written by the bourgeoisie for the bourgeoisie [...] you have a generation of working-class people who have never known the habit of going to the theatre, who have been totally intimidated, who would never dare to presume to go to these places [...] in the twenties – and thirties and forties – you still had this middle-class stranglehold on the theatre, excluding whole sections of our society." (Jones, 1989, pp. 21–22)

His ideas changed dramatically when his girlfriend, now his wife, took him to Liverpool's Everyman Theatre. The experience is echoed by Rita's enthusiasm for her first visit to the theatre. At that time, in the early seventies, regional drama was being encouraged by a group of young directors in some major northern English cities. Russell commented, "They turned it into a real local people's theatre [...]. The working class voice was allowed to be heard" (*The Independent*, 23. 1. 88). This experience showed him what kind of things he wanted to write and made him decide to study drama at a teacher's training college. But first, at the age of twenty, he had to start taking O-level and A -level exams and raise the money to pay for his studies. His reasons for returning to full-time education were similar to Rita's – he "wanted to know everything", to catch up on all the culture he had missed. And so he recommenced his education at St Katharine's College of Education. When he left in 1973 he started work as a teacher, but the success of his play *John, Paul, George, Ringo and Bert* in 1974, about Russell's experiences as a 14-year-old Beatles fan, enabled him to give up teaching and become a full-time writer.

During his studies Russell had decided that he wanted to write for working class audiences. Indeed, he is remarkable because no other British playwright has ever had such a series of successes all dealing with the lives of the working class. He is one of a group of left-wing Merseyside writers which has recently emerged and which has been immensely popular in the theatre, television and film. Almost every theatre in Britain has staged *Educating Rita*. It was written in 1979 and first performed a year later in London. In 1983 it was made into a film with the close collaboration of Russell himself.

Educating Rita is a passionate plea for everyone's right to a decent education. Russell feels strongly that the working class is being denied access to many aspects of the national culture. Their limited access to cultural products is partly due to expectations about their tastes and abilities. But it is also partly a result of their own attitudes. Russell differs from many other writers on "working class culture" in that he does not romanticise about it, but exposes bigotry and resistance to change. Rita illustrates a theme found in many of his major plays since the mid-1970s: someone driven by a sense of frustration fights for an education that will help them to break through the limitations of the class and culture into which they were born.

Educating Rita also expresses Russell's resentment towards those who believe that art is only for a highly educated minority. He attacks the elitism of what he describes as the "literature industry", consisting of an opera industry, a theatre industry and many who work in these fields, such as producers, directors, the editors of theatre magazines and critics:

> "There's something I call the 'literature industry' which has sprung up and which I particularly loathe because it seems to me to put a huge barrier between the Ritas of this world who want to learn and literature itself. It probably comes out in my own sort of situation; for years and years and years I wouldn't pick a classical or known and regarded author from the bookshelves. I'd rather read a racy, accessible American novel or indeed quality American novels because they were rarely classified as literature [...]. [I'm] trying to attack the divisions really in teaching, in education, and in the class system. And so it's the division and it's the elitist way in which literature is dealt with that I really object to." (Glaap, 1984, pp. 21–22)

Russell describes his aim in writing *Educating Rita* as follows, "I wanted to make a play which engaged and was relevant to those who had no knowledge of literature, those who considered themselves uneducated, those whose daily language is not the language of the university or the theatre" (Glaap, 1984, p. 5). A comment in *The Independent* newspaper (23. 1. 88) verifies that Russell's plays "are still aimed [...] at the kind of people whose hair he cut". Interestingly, despite his fame, Russell has remained in Liverpool, refusing to move to London partly out of fear that he would be sucked into the middle classes.

Some of Russell's Most Important Plays

John, Paul, George, Ringo and Bert 1974
Breezeblock Park 1975
Our Day Out 1977
Educating Rita (stage) 1980
Blood Brothers 1983
Educating Rita (film) 1983
Shirley Valentine 1986

The Plot

Dr Frank Bryant, a university lecturer in his early fifties, needs some extra money to pay for his drinking habit, so he agrees to tutor an Open University student. The Open University is a government programme for adults who go back to education later in life, for example women who have had children. It was founded in 1969 and opened up higher education to a broader section of the population. Teaching is by a mixture of printed materials, television and radio programmes. Each student is given a tutor, like Frank, whom they see regularly. He sets them tasks, they post him their work and he marks it and discusses it with them.

Frank is confronted with Rita, a brash twenty-six-year-old Liverpudlian hairdresser. Although she is very intelligent, she did not get much of an education at school, largely because in the working class area where she was brought up school achievement was regarded as an attempt to be better than everyone else. Yet despite her poor education she has a mind of her own and expresses her opinions honestly and spontaneously.

Rita has always felt that there was more to life than the everyday routine. She realises that her poor education stands in the way of a better quality life. Eventually she becomes so unhappy that she decides to acquire that education. She explains to Frank that she wants to find out what she has missed. She wants, for instance, to be able to make more informed choices about art and literature instead of simply rejecting "highbrow" culture automatically because it is not part of traditional working class life. In fact, she wants nothing less than a whole education, "a better culture".

Rita finds her working class environment narrow and confining. She suffers from a lack of mental stimulation and is frustrated with the inflexible attitudes of those around her. No one understands why she cannot settle for the traditional role of wife and mother. She suspects that people feel threatened by her desire for change, as if she were rejecting their lifestyles and values. Signing on for the Open University course was a difficult decision because she knew that education would change her and may even alienate her from her present environment. But her desire for change is so strong that she is prepared to take the risk.

Rita is alert, observant and eager to learn. She loves literature, and has even changed her name from Susan to Rita in admiration of a popular novel by Rita Mae Brown, *Rubyfruit Jungle* (1973). This novel is about an independent minded, culture-hungry woman called Molly Bolt, a woman, in fact, just like Rita herself. But Rita's approach is naive and she cannot discriminate between writers of acknowledged good quality and popular fiction. Frank finds her enthusiasm refreshing, but sees that her reactions are highly subjective and that she is completely ignorant of the accepted code of literary criticism. He realises that in order to pass exams she will have to suppress her spontaneous, emotional response to literature. He is aware of the danger that she might become like his other students, who give him the conventional, second-hand opinions of literary critics rather than their own feelings. Because he does not want Rita to lose her originality Frank tries to dissuade her from taking the course. But she insists.

Rita's home life gradually becomes more and more difficult. She had enrolled for the course against her husband, Denny's, wishes. He takes a traditional view of the role of women and wants her to stop taking the pill and have a child. He cannot understand her need for better choices in life. He himself is content if he is offered eight different kinds of beer. As Rita describes the situation at home to Frank she attacks the system which denies working class people meaningful choices of what to do with their lives.

Frank precipitates a crisis when he invites Rita and Denny to a dinner party. Denny refuses, but Rita sets out alone. Standing outside Frank's house she looks in through the window and realises that she cannot go in. She has become a cultural misfit, alienated from her working class environment, but not belonging to Frank's world either. Sadly, she joins her family in the pub. She has already decided to give her studies up when her mother starts crying and makes a remark which shows how disappointed she is with her own life. This changes Rita's mind. She becomes even more determined not to become trapped like her mother.

When Denny finds out that Rita is still taking the pill, against his wishes, he burns her books and gives her the ultimatum of either giving the course up or leaving home. But by now Rita's studies have become so important to her that they represent life itself. She can no more give them up than she can stop breathing. So she moves out.

Half way through the play Rita attends a summer school in London and comes back a changed person, outwardly and inwardly. She has become much more self-confident and has learned a lot about her subject. To Frank's dismay she has already read the poems of William Blake. Her reactions to them prove Frank's worst fears. She has learned to discuss literature in controlled, analytic terms and her spontaneous, passionate reactions to it have been suppressed. Rita has now found the "better culture" she was seeking. She copies the lifestyles and opinions of educated people around her, such as her flatmate, Trish. But as Rita becomes more knowledgeable, Frank falls into an even deeper depression. For a while she had given his teaching some meaning, a sense of purpose. He had come to depend on her visits. But now the old Rita has practically disappeared and the new one no longer needs him. There are whole areas of her life about which he knows nothing. She had not told him, for instance, about her new flatmate or about her change of job. He is so disappointed that he even tells her he will be glad to see her leave. Gradually, their positions are reversed: Rita turns into an academic, skillfully applying the analytic methods of literary criticism which Frank has taught her, whilst he himself longs for emotional responses to the literature he loves.

After summer school the relationship between Frank and Rita changes dramatically. More and more, we feel that they are exchanging places. For whereas Rita is asserting her independence from her tutor, he is growing increasingly dependent on her. At one time Frank was Rita's only hope, but now she seems to be the only person he can relate to. But their old familiarity has gone. He is no longer the focal point of her life. She is forming other relationships and hardly shows any personal interest in him at all any more. Besides, she is now more interested in art and literature than in other people. As she becomes an "expert" on literature, the originality and honesty which once distinguished her from the average student are buried by conventional, second-hand opinions.

The depths of Frank's despair are revealed when he turns up drunk for a lecture and makes some bitter, ironic comments on the literary establishment, including himself as part of it. Rita's development has made him even more aware of how destructive traditional methods of teaching literature can be. Eventually his new preference for subjective, emotional responses, together with his drinking, lead to his taking a forced sabbatical.

Things come to a head between Frank and Rita when he asks for her opinion on some of his poems. Instead of giving him her honest, personal reactions, she repeats the complicated, pretentious interpretation of her flatmate. Frank is bitterly disappointed. During the ensuing quarrel he suggests that Rita's new-found "culture" is superficial and that all she is doing is imitating others. She accuses him, and the middle classes altogether, of preferring the working class to remain uneducated so that they can be patronised. After this all contact between Rita and her tutor seems to stop until Frank tries to ring her about her exam. This is when he finds out something else she had not told him, that she has reverted to her original name of Susan.

After the exam, Frank is packing for Australia when Rita returns to thank him. Finally she has realised that he was right. She had been so hungry for education and culture that she had accepted the lifestyles and opinions of educated people unquestioningly. Now she realises that Frank had been warning her not to be taken in by appearances and to try to retain her honesty and spontaneity. She has also been affected by the attempted suicide of her flatmate, Trish, on whom she had modelled herself. Under Trish's veneer of culture her life had really been empty and meaningless. Rita understands now that to lead a more meaningful life she must do more than talk about literature and copy educated people.

Frank recognises the old Rita and asks her to accompany him to Australia. But Rita has only just begun to take control of her own life and does not want to be pressed into making any decisions yet. There are several alternatives, but it does not seem to matter which one she chooses. With her new confidence and skills, she has achieved her aim of acquiring a better quality of personal choices. She has also managed to balance the old Rita, the hairdresser, with Susan, the educated woman. After a period of simply exchanging one set of conventions for another, she has now rediscovered her independence of mind. For her, education has been a liberating experience, after all.

Act I, Scene 1
Rita goes to see her Open University tutor, Dr Frank Bryant. She explains what she wants from the course. Frank is reluctant to teach her.

Act I, Scene 2
Rita needs to change her subjective approach to literature. She tells Frank about her school days.

Act I, Scene 3
Rita has to become more discriminating in her reading.

Act I, Scene 4
Denny does not like Rita's studying. Rita explains her views on "working class culture". She finally understands the meaning of Forster's phrase "only connect".

Act I, Scene 5
Denny burns Rita's books. Frank explains why he stopped writing poetry. Rita persuades Frank to go with her to see her first play.

Act I, Scene 6
Rita is so overwhelmed by *Macbeth* that she has to tell Frank about it. Frank invites Rita and Denny to a dinner party.

Act I, Scene 7
Rita did not turn up at Frank's dinner party. She feels like a social misfit. Her mother's regret makes her determined to go on with her education.

Act I, Scene 8
Denny has thrown Rita out. Her essay on *Macbeth* is still too emotional. Frank is unwilling to change her way of thinking, but she insists.

Act II, Scene 1
After summer school Rita is more self-confident. She no longer informs Frank about changes in her life, such as her new flatmate. She even tries to influence him. He realises that she is losing her originality. Frank and Rita seem to be exchanging places: Frank is looking for a direct, emotional reaction to literature, while she discusses it in a more detached manner.

Act II, Scene 2
Rita is very much influenced by Trish. She feels that at last she has found "a better culture". Frank is afraid that she will regard the opinions of literary authorities as absolute truths. Now she is writing the same kind of essay as his other students.

Act II, Scene 3
Frank has been reported for drunkenness. He criticises Rita's work for being full of borrowed ideas, but admits that it would get a good mark in an exam. She feels she no longer needs his guidance.

Act II, Scene 4
Rita has not told Frank about her change of job. She prefers to talk about more interesting things with people who are "not trapped". They quarrel and Frank suggests that she can no longer see what really matters in life. He asks for her opinion on some of his poems.

Act II, Scene 5
Frank is bitterly disappointed with Rita's second-hand judgements of his poems. Sarcastically, he suggests that he has created a monster. Rita accuses him of taking his education for granted.

Act II, Scene 6
Frank and Rita now have so little contact that he has to ring her at work to give her the details of her exam. He does not know, either, that she has reverted to her original name of Susan.

Act II, Scene 7
Frank has been advised to take a two year sabbatical. He is packing for Australia when Rita comes back to thank him and tell him that he was right. She had mistaken the veneer of culture for real education. Trish's attempted suicide also showed her that there is more to life than art and literature. For the first time in her life, she has real, meaningful choices.

Analysis and Interpretation

Act I, Scene 1

The play opens with Dr Frank Bryant in his study at the university where he is Senior Lecturer in English. He is searching among the books on his shelves. Then he finds what he was looking for, a bottle of whisky hidden behind one of the books. He has just taken his first drink when the phone rings. From the conversation we gather that he is speaking to a woman, probably his wife or girlfriend. It becomes clear that their relationship is not very harmonious, probably because she does not like his drinking. We also learn that Frank is waiting for an Open University student. From the phone conversation we conclude that Frank is witty, with a taste for irony.

The phone call is interrupted by someone knocking at the door. Although he repeatedly invites his visitor to come in, the knocking continues. Eventually his new student, Rita, bursts into the room. She is annoyed and reproaches Frank about the door handle, which needs mending. Frank is taken aback by this unconventional entrance. When he asks Rita for her name she does not understand his question "You are?" She is obviously not used to formal situations. From Rita's first appearance we conclude that she is a very open, direct sort of person.

As the scene progresses Rita explains why she wants to take the Open University course. For a long time she has been feeling "out of step" with everyone around her, as if she were dancing to a different tune. At twenty-six everyone is surprised that she has not yet had a baby. She has lied to her husband, telling him that she is no longer taking the pill, but she herself does not want a child yet. First she feels the need to "discover" herself. Neither her husband nor her neighbours and friends would be able to understand this. When she tries to explain to her husband that she wants a change, all he can suggest is moving house. Rita feels starved of intellectual stimulation and has decided to try to discover and develop the potential which she feels is inside her. She is aware that this process will involve very deep changes, not the superficial ones which she sees every day at the hairdresser's where she works. She criticises her customers for thinking that changing their hairstyles will somehow transform them into new individuals. Yet, although she says she sometimes hates these women, she also understands that their limited horizons are a result of their poor education. Like these women, Rita has already begun to change in a very superficial way. She was so impressed by a novel written by Rita Mae Brown that she decided to call herself Rita, instead of Susan (White). She knows, though, that real growth must come from within and involve the whole personality.

At present Rita feels imprisoned by the fixed habits and attitudes of the working class people around her. They cling on to what they know and automatically reject anything new, without even trying to understand it. For instance they reject "highbrow" art forms, such as ballet and opera, labelling them as "posh" and "middle class". Rita finds this kind of intolerance limiting. She imagines that a better education will liberate her from such conventional attitudes and enable her to form her own judgements. But first she needs to find out more about "highbrow" culture. A course in literature seems to be a good starting point. She envies Frank's ability to make conscious choices about which books to read and which TV programmes to watch and longingly asks him what it is like to be free. Russell himself answered the question of what the Open University course means to Rita in an interview, "She does want to be able to sit down and discuss books and art and music and to be spiritually fed and, to stay in the metaphor, she feels that she's starving in her present social stratum, that it's arid and that if she moves in this other stratum it will be some sort of oasis" (Glaap, 1984, p. 95).

Typical 1970s working class housing for people like Rita

Rita's remarks on culture suggest that the working class tend to prefer "lowbrow" or "popular" entertainment which is relatively easy to understand, whereas educated middle class people like Frank prefer something more "highbrow". In comparison with Frank, Rita is much more aware of the link between social class, education and cultural tastes. She herself reads indiscriminately and is unaware of any difference between good quality literature and popular pulp fiction. Several humorous misunderstandings arise because of the different levels of knowledge and education. Rita, for instance, thinks that when Frank mentions Yeats, the poet, he is referring to Yates, the wine shop, which is pronounced in the same way. And when she talks about Elliot, she means Elliott Ness, a Chicago policeman, and not the famous poet, T. S. Eliot.

These misunderstandings show Rita how much she needs to learn about literature if she wants to take the Open University exams. She is still a little unsure about taking the course, although she is deadly serious about wanting to learn. She explains that despite her brash manner she really lacks self-confidence. The only thing which prevents her from giving the whole thing up and going home is Frank's personality. She had obviously been expecting a different type of person and admits that she used bad language in order to "test" him. But because he did not object to her swearing she feels accepted. He does not seem to want to force his own standards on her. Rita finally decides to stay because she likes her tutor. Having made such a difficult decision, her disappointment is acute when Frank suddenly announces that he is no longer willing to teach her. He had only taken the OU course on because of the extra money. Meeting Rita confirms his suspicion that he has made a mistake. He explains that he is not a good teacher, but that this does not matter to the majority of his students. He sees, however, that Rita is different because she expects so much more – she wants to learn "everything". Her total ignorance about literary analysis means that he will have to explain things he would normally take for granted. He knows that her thirst for knowledge and also her honesty will not allow her to accept anything she does not understand. This is demonstrated when Rita asks him what "assonance" means, a word she had picked up from some students on the way to his room. He has obviously never really thought about it and the example he gives is, to her, "getting the rhyme wrong". Frank is amused and disarmed by her simple, honest response. He finds her a refreshing change from his other students. Unlike them, she has a genuine love of literature and responds to it directly and spontaneously. Her total ignorance of literary traditions and analysis prevents her from repeating second-hand ideas. It is apparently a long time since he has had such an enthusiastic student. It also seems a long time since he has felt any sense of purpose or fulfilment in his teaching.

Surprisingly, Frank does not immediately grasp this rare opportunity to share his love of his subject and develop Rita's mind. Instead, he refuses to teach her. Knowing how much the course means to her he feels he is not capable of fulfilling her expectations. Also, he probably shies away from so much responsibility. But Rita refuses to be turned away, insisting that he has agreed to teach her and this is what he must do. As she walks out we are uncertain

as to whether she will really come back and, if she does, whether Frank will accept her or not.
This first meeting makes it clear that Rita is not a typical university student. Despite her poor education she has a very independent mind. Her approach to literature is fresh because she has not yet been taught to repeat second-hand opinions about it in order to pass exams. She expresses her opinions honestly and spontaneously. Despite the huge differences between Rita and Frank, they also have something in common, for they are both unhappy and frustrated with their lives and the cultures they belong to. Paradoxically, both try to escape to each other's worlds. Rita sees in Frank the key to a better, freer life and aspires to become "cultured", like him. However, Frank despises his way of life and finds his middle class, academic environment shallow and pretentious. Rita's unspoiled mind shows him all the more clearly how fragile his own assumptions are. To him she is the first breath of fresh air which has been in his room for years. We sense that he would like to revert to some stage before his literary education began, when his reactions to literature were still like Rita's, unspoiled by received literary opinions.

Act I, Scene 2

Frank is in his study, obviously expecting someone, when he sees the door handle being turned. Since no one enters, he pulls the door open. To his surprise Rita is standing outside, oiling the handle. It seems that their conflict has been resolved. Either they have been in touch with each other or Frank has gradually got used to the idea of teaching her, for the question is no longer discussed. As Rita looks out of the window at the students on the lawns she wistfully tells Frank that as a child she always wanted to go to a public school. From Frank's horrified response we gather that he dislikes the elitism of these institutions. Asked why she did not go on to university after school, Rita explains that in the working class area where she lived nobody expected her to learn. Taking school seriously would have meant being different from her friends and this was "not allowed". She would have been an outsider. And so, like the other girls, she concentrated instead on music, clothes and boys and finally got married. But she always felt that there was something missing in her life, until one day she admitted to herself that she was extremely unhappy. This was the point where she had to decide whether to go on pretending and compensate for her unhappiness with new dresses or whether to try to make a new start. The decision was very hard because it meant that she would have to change. She knew that no one would understand her and that she would become alienated from her environment.
Abruptly Rita stops talking and turns to the essay which she has written for Frank on *Rubyfruit Jungle*. This is where Rita's first lesson in literary criticism

begins. Instead of analysing the novel in an objective way she has simply described it and given her personal reactions. Her opinion of E. M. Forster's novel *Howards End* (1910) is similarly subjective – "crap". She rejects it because the author took no account of the conditions of the poor at the time of writing. Frank is astounded at so much subjectivity and that Rita judges works of art on whether they relate to real life or not. He explains that the orthodox way of writing literary appreciation is to be objective and to support opinions with references to accepted authorities.

However, Rita's undisciplined mind is finding it difficult to concentrate. Suddenly she starts asking Frank personal questions. He is exasperated, but Rita has a great natural curiosity about people and cannot be put off. To satisfy her, Frank tells her he has split up from his wife and is now living with a former student, Julia. His remarks about both women are bitterly sarcastic. We also learn that Frank has a low opinion of himself and finds himself shallow. Nevertheless, Rita envies his "educated" way of expressing himself. Her naiveté astonishes Frank and again he realises how much he will have to teach her.

Rita is disappointed when he tries to turn the conversation back to *Howards End*. She is reminded of her school days, when teachers often killed off interesting subjects by over-analysing them. Frank's remark that this is what education does earns him a rebuke. Education is so valuable to Rita that she cannot see how anyone could possibly criticise it. She challenges him to explain why he is giving her an education if he is so unsure of its value. Frank's answer is less than convincing, "Because it's what you want". His comment that he would actually prefer to take her by the hand and run out of the room forever is partly an attempt to lighten the tone of the conversation, but also partly serious. Rita has let some light and air into his boring, routine existence and it is understandable that he really would like to escape from it all with her.

Rita cannot see that Frank is not merely paying her compliments. She is blind to the cry of despair behind his question "Rita – why didn't you walk in here twenty years ago?" Someone like her could have saved him. He might still be writing poetry, might even have achieved greatness instead of doing a job which was becoming more and more meaningless. Eventually Frank realises that Rita needs him to teach her – him and no one else. In a tone half determined, half angry, he warns her that she will have to work hard and that if she is not prepared to do this she might as well give up already. But Rita has no intention of giving up, nor is she cowed. Once more, she completely disarms him, remarking how impressive he looks when he is angry.

It is highly significant that Rita has to study E. M. Forster's *Howards End*. Like her, the hero, Leonard Bast, comes from the working class and is trying to educate himself, although he lives in poverty. He, too, realises that there is more to life than day to day existence. He loves literature and music, but is living with a woman who cannot understand him. By chance, Leonard gets to know a wealthy, cultured family. At first he denies his humble origins and tries to copy the culture of the upper class, but eventually he progresses beyond mere imitation.

Act I, Scene 3

Rita is working on E. M. Forster's novel *Howards End*, but is having great difficulty understanding it, especially his now famous phrase "only connect". Frank cannot accept her essay on it because of all the references to popular fiction. Rita feels this is unfair because, after all, he had told her to refer to other authors. But Frank had forgotten Rita's inability to distinguish between "good quality" literature and pulp fiction. He had taken it for granted that she would only refer to accepted literary authorities. To Rita all books are "literature". When she asks Frank to explain the difference he is confused and embarrassed. It is obvious that he has taken over traditional ideas about what constitutes "good" literature without really giving the question much thought. Despite his embarrassment, Frank finds Rita refreshing because her reactions to literature have not been shaped by other people. His students and colleagues, on the other hand, are probably no longer able to react to literature in such a direct, honest way because they know what the approved, orthodox reactions should be. From Frank's reaction Rita draws the conclusion that she should stop reading popular fiction. However, he explains that she can go on reading it, as long as she is aware of its position in the literary hierarchy, that it is not usually analysed for its literary qualities, but simply read for enjoyment.

Act I, Scene 4

Rita is still having problems with the phrase, "only connect", with which Forster introduced his novel *Howards End*. By the end of the scene she has understood it and we see how relevant it is for her own development.

Rita cannot work at home because her husband is against her studying. So to avoid arguments she writes her essays at the hairdressing salon. Of course, if they are busy she does not have much time, which partly accounts for the brevity of her essay on the difficulties of staging Ibsen's play *Peer Gynt* (1876). (Again, Russell's choice of this particular play is significant, since it is about someone who is searching for the meaning of life). In fact, her essay only consisted of the one sentence, "Do it on the radio". When Frank confronts her about it her explanation completely disarms him because it shows that she has understood Ibsen's intentions very well. She argues that since he wrote it as a play for voices, he would have solved the staging difficulties by presenting it as a radio play if this medium had existed. Once again, Frank is impressed by the originality of Rita's thinking. Nevertheless, he realises that he still has a lot of work to do. In order to pass exams she must learn – and be willing to accept – the orthodox method of writing essays on literature.

Scene 4 is particularly important because of Rita's opinions on working class culture. Russell is certainly using her as a mouthpiece when she denies the existence of a specific working class culture. (See Theme 1 for further details). Her view is that although the working class think they have culture, there is no real meaning to their lives, even though materially speaking they might be quite well off. (Today the situation is different. The old working class has divided into a new working class with a somewhat higher status and an impoverished underclass). Rita describes a vicious circle of frustration and compensation through consumer goods. She feels that the working class is manipulated by the mass media and that their choices in life, although many, are really very narrow – quantity as opposed to quality. This reflects the author's own conviction that the working class is deprived of good quality choices.

As Rita speaks, Frank notes her understanding of the underlying structures of society and asks why she did not study politics instead of literature. Rita, however, hates politics, probably because she feels that politicians are not interested in changing the situation of the working class in any fundamental way. Frank uses Rita's description of the vicious circle of working class life to demonstrate to her that she does indeed understand Forster's phrase "only connect", but was not aware of how it related to herself. This is an important step in Rita's development because it makes her more conscious of how various phenomena are interrelated. It will help her to think in a more structured way.

Asked why he did not simply tell her what Forster's phrase meant from the beginning, Frank explains that he prefers to allow her to find things out for herself. We begin to suspect that he is a much better teacher than he himself believes.

Frank's suggestion that there is nothing wrong with working class life as long as people are happy shows that he does not know anything about the working class. Furthermore, he is not interested in them. Here Russell is illustrating the barriers which exist between the classes. He is also implying that the better educated do not care about those less privileged than themselves.

Act I, Scene 5

Rita arrives for her tutorial without an essay which she was supposed to write. Denny found out that she was secretly on the pill and was so angry that he burned her books and papers, including the essay. He cannot understand why she does not want a child yet and feels that she is denying him his right to have children. In the previous scene Rita told Frank that Denny had tried to stop her attending her tutorial, wanting her to go out with him and his friends instead. Rita believes he feels threatened because she is trying to break away from the traditional working class way of life. He cannot understand her desire for more meaningful choices in life than materialistic ones such as eight different kinds of beer. She told her husband that she would have a baby if and when she chose to. Rita understands Denny's feelings and is sorry for him. She knows that he is so fixed in his ways and in his thinking that he is incapable of understanding her needs. He must feel that she has in some way betrayed him by changing into a different person.

In view of the seriousness of the situation Frank would prefer to discuss Rita's future. But she explains that she can no more give up her studies than she can give up breathing. The course represents life itself to her, she lives for nothing else. She tells Frank that he gives her "room to breathe", that he "feeds her". At this Frank warns that art and literature should not become more important than real life. Rita, however, insists on going on with the tutorial. She has made the decision to continue her education, even though it may cost her her marriage. More than ever before Frank realises just how much it means to her and what the cost might be. He had never really understood how much she had been up against. And now she needs help which only he can give.

Characteristically, Rita changes the subject and asks Frank why he stopped writing poetry. He explains that instead of writing poetry he spent years trying to create "literature". By this he means the sort of work which would be acceptable to literary critics and could be studied and "appreciated" by students. He further confuses Rita by his comment that people should not believe in literature. Here Russell himself is speaking. The author is highly critical of what he calls the "literature industry" and of the elitist way in which literature is dealt with. He questions the absolute status of great authors, which is created by this "literature industy. (See Theme 3 for more details). Frank's explanation suggests that he drinks in order to suppress his frustration about his teaching, his poetry, the way literature is dealt with by the so-called "experts" and his personal life.

Act I, Scene 6

Rita bursts into Frank's study, breathless and excited. He is alarmed, imagining that something serious has happened. And it has. Seeing *Macbeth* on stage was a major event in Rita's life. She is still so overwhelmed by the experience that she has to tell someone about it and Frank is the only person she thinks will understand. She had expected Shakespeare to be boring, but had "wanted to find out". This is reminiscent of the reason she gave for starting the course in scene 1, "I wanna know". She wants to find out what she has missed through not having had a good education.

Frank takes the opportunity to explain what "tragedy" means in dramatic terms. Rita learns that it is different from the so-called "tragedies" reported in the type of newspapers she reads. She is surprised that there is so much more to *Macbeth* than just an exciting story. But she is also dismayed because she realises how ignorant she is about literature and the academic code. Her reactions to literature are still limited to a purely emotional response.

Rita's first visit to a "proper" theatre echoes an important event in the author's own life. When he first started going to the theatre it seemed very far removed from his own working class background. Then, in the early seventies, things changed. A group of young directors in some northern English cities were beginning to encourage new, local playwrights and this marked a turning-point for Russell. He enjoyed this new type of play so much that he started studying drama and decided to write plays especially for working class people like himself.

As Rita is leaving to go back to the hairdressing salon Frank invites her to a dinner party at his house. She is stunned. Why should he invite her? What could she possibly contribute? What does he want of her? Surprised, he simply suggests that she might enjoy it. This was an aspect she had not considered. When Frank extends the invitation to include Denny, Rita has a mental picture of her husband among Frank's guests. She already knows that he will refuse.

Act I, Scene 7

When Rita appears for her next tutorial she is confronted by an angry Frank. She and Denny had not turned up at his dinner party and Rita's only explanation had been a brief note of apology which she had scribbled on the back of her essay and put through his letter box. She explains that Denny had refused to go and they had quarrelled. So she had set off alone. It had been difficult to find the house, but eventually she had arrived outside Frank's door. Through the window she could see him and his guests talking and laughing. Suddenly she realised she could not go in. She had brought the wrong sort of wine and was probably wearing the wrong clothes. But, above all, she was afraid of making a fool of herself. The only way she could join in the conversation would be to amuse them all by her witty remarks. But she did not want to "play the court jester", as she puts it. She wanted to be taken seriously, to be accepted on their terms. So she had written the note and gone to join her family in the pub.

Rita and her family's kind of pub

Frank reproaches Rita for upsetting Julia's arrangements, but we suspect that really he was very disappointed. Because he himself is so fascinated by her he imagines that everyone else will find her equally delightful. He had not stopped to consider the embarrassing position he had put Rita in. This lack of understanding once again shows that he is completely unaware of the difficulties facing people from her background. After suggesting that she should see a psychiatrist he asks why she does not simply give the course up if it is causing so many problems. Why not just stay with her family and join in the singing in the pub? Rita has to explain that it is impossible for her to revert to her former life. She has begun to find out what was missing and can no longer stop. She did try to join in with the singing, but it was no good. She is in a no man's land, trapped between two worlds. Her old life has slipped away, but a new one is not yet in reach.

As Rita sat among her singing relatives in the pub her mother started to cry. When Rita asked what was wrong she explained, "because we could sing better songs than those". Denny chose to ignore his mother-in-law's unhappiness and cheered her up again. He prefers a facade of happiness to the truth because facing up to problems usually means making some kind of changes. But Denny does not have the courage for that.

Rita sees that her mother is disappointed and frustrated with the emptiness of her life, but cannot do anything about it. Through the contrasts with her mother and Denny we see even more clearly how difficult it is for Rita to break away, to sing her own song. Rita sees her mother's tears as a warning not to become trapped, too, and becomes even more determined to give her own life as much meaning as she can by creating better choices for herself.

Act I, Scene 8

Rita comes into Frank's study, carrying a suitcase. Denny has issued the ultimatum that she must either give up her studies and stop taking the pill or leave. He feels she is betraying him and his social origins – also her own – by rejecting the traditional working class way of life. He seems to need her to live by the accepted code in order to reinforce and justify his own values. Rita understands him and concedes that from his point of view he is right. But it is more important to her not to betray herself. She feels she must try to live up to her potential.

Rita has arranged to stay with her parents until she finds a flat. But first she needs to see Frank. With her life disintegrating around her he is the only remaining fixed point. She rejects his attempt to comfort her and insists on discussing her essay on *Macbeth*. Now, more than ever, she needs to feel that some part of her life is solid and valuable.

Frank is bewildered. He would like to comfort and help her, but she will only accept what he can give her as a teacher. What should he say? Her essay is powerful and moving, but far too emotional for exam purposes. To pass exams she would have to change, he would have to change her. And he is not at all sure that he wants to do that because he would risk suppressing her honesty and spontaneity. He might completely destroy her uniqueness. Her independent mind might become full of second-hand opinions and literary jargon.

Rita cannot see Frank's problem at all. After all, she wants to change. That was the whole point of taking the course. She begins to wonder if he is trying to tell her gently that she is not good enough. When he reassures her about that she comes to another conclusion, that he probably finds it too difficult to teach someone like her, with her untutored mind and her background. She explains that criticism will not hurt her feelings. On the contrary, she needs him to set clear standards, otherwise she cannot realise her ambition of writing essays and passing exams like all his other students.

By the end of Act I the play has reached a climax. Rita's marriage has broken up and she has become alienated from her original environment. Now she can only go forward. To make it all worthwhile she must fulfil her ambition of joining the ranks of the educated, learning their codes, speaking their language, knowing which kind of wine to buy. First she has to come up to the same standard as the other students, which she must prove by passing the same exams. We wonder whether she will manage all this without, as Frank fears, losing too much of her uniqueness.

Act II, Scene 1

As part of her Open University course Rita has attended a summer school in London. She bursts into Frank's study to tell him about it. Outwardly, she has altered her style of dressing and Frank soon realises that she has also changed in other, less superficial ways. London itself offered many new experiences and on the course she met new people and learned more about her subject. She has obviously become more self-confident about expressing her views on literature and is particularly proud of the first time she asked a question in front of a lecture-room full of people.

After relating her experiences she enquires about Frank's holiday in France. From his brief, hesitant remarks we conclude that it was not too successful. Then he explains that Julia left him, although she has since returned. Frank gathers from Rita's conversation that she has a new friend, Trish. Although he does not say anything he must feel hurt that Rita no longer tells him everything. Rita obviously admires Trish for her culture and good taste. She embodies everything Rita ever wanted. She tells Frank how much she is enjoying her present life and how she feels young and alive again among her fellow-students.

When Rita gives Frank a present of a pen solely for writing poetry his thanks are rather subdued, probably because he resents this attempt to influence him. Rita then suggests that they discuss next term's work outside on the grass, but Frank refuses. So she tries to let some air in through the window. We are reminded of their first meeting, when Frank saw her as the first breath of fresh air that had been in his stuffy, academic room for years. But now, significantly, the window will not open. The refreshing, irreverent Rita of the beginning has disappeared and the new one cannot let any fresh air in. She is gradually turning into a "normal" student, just like all the others.

As Frank takes his whisky bottle from its hiding place Rita reproaches him for drinking so much. This is new, too. She never used to try to change him, but accepted him as he was. He wonders what would happen if he agreed to reform, to please her, and then she left. Where would he be then? Rita is taken aback. She lives so much in the present that she has not thought about the time after her exams. She is shocked when Frank says that not only is her going inevitable, but that he will actually be pleased when she leaves. He sees that she is hurt by his comment and does not have the heart to explain. So he reassures her by lightly brushing it aside. But he was serious. He knows that as she becomes an "expert" on literature he will dislike her more and more. But he also knows that she would not understand his fears and that, in

any case, he can no longer stop her from becoming a "proper" student, with all that this entails.
Instead, he tells her about a poet he had been saving up for her. He obviously loves William Blake and is looking forward to Rita's reactions. He expects her to see the poems as he does, without over-complicating them. Rita astonishes him by reciting one of Blake's poems from memory. She "did" him at summer school. Frank feels as if he has been robbed of his most precious possession. He had been saving this gift up, looking forward to the time when he could help her to understand him properly, in the way that most literary critics did not. And now his gift is not appreciated. Rita is not aware of his dismay as she proves to him how much she knows about Blake. As he listens, Frank realises that to her Blake is just another poet, to be ticked off as part of a course on English literature. She had been introduced to him before she was ready and by someone who knew nothing about her and was not concerned about her progress. She should not have read Blake without him.
The incident about Blake suggests that Frank and Rita are gradually beginning to exchange places. Whilst Rita discusses the poems in the sophisticated manner of a student of literature, Frank's reaction is a more direct, emotional one, rather like Rita's approach to literature when they first met.
It is interesting that Russell chose William Blake's two sets of poems, *Songs of Innocence and Experience* for Rita to study at summer school. The first set, *Songs of Innocence*, begun in 1789, is about childlike innocence and ideals, whereas the *Songs of Experience* (1794) are often bitter as they describe how these ideals turn into illusions. The poem which Rita recites, "The Sick Rose", is one of the *Songs of Experience*. Russell's choice of Blake's collection symbolises Rita's progress from innocence to experience as she learns more about literature and literary criticism. But it can also be seen as a warning that her dreams may turn sour.

Act II, Scene 2

Rita is late for her class. When she finally arrives she speaks in an unnatural, upper-middle class voice. Apparently Trish finds Rita's way of speaking ugly and is trying to persuade her to talk "properly". Frank does not seem too pleased that Rita has found another mentor. Again and again he notices how she tries to imitate her new flatmate. In fact, Trish has opened up a whole new way of life to Rita. At long last she has been admitted to a world of books, plants and the "right" furniture, a world in which people know which wines to buy. Finally she has acquired "a better culture". Rita's mention of plants is significant because it echoes something in Russell's own life. In an interview he once described his family background:

> "I came from a house in which we wouldn't have a plant, we wouldn't have a picture, we wouldn't sit at a table, we'd have food on our knees whilst watching telly. So when I first moved into a different world, before I went to college, and started to mix with people, I'd go into people's houses and they'd have all these things – they didn't live their lives for things, it was just a natural expression of their sensibilities on the whole. One used to want not the pictures, not the plants but what one saw as the ritual way of living. A calmer, more fulfilling life. It's only later on that you find out that is just a particular veneer and that life can be just as arid, if you think it will be better if you have the right pictures on the wall and the right plants." (Jones, 1989, p. 334)

This description makes it clear that *Educating Rita* is partly a description of Russell's own attempt to acquire a "better culture".

Rita's excuse for being late was that she had been unavoidably delayed, but a few minutes later she says she actually arrived early and was talking to some students. Frank notes that her tutorials used to be far too important for her to arrive late, but says nothing. He only expresses surprise that she had the courage to address other, "proper" students. The fact that she no longer stands in awe of them shows how much she has gained in both knowledge and self-confidence. She even boasts to Frank about how she corrected one of the students.

Frank realises just how much she has changed. She has indeed learned to recognise what is normally classed as "good" literature – he had taught her himself – but now she proclaims her judgements as absolute truths. How can he explain to her that people still have the right to their own preferences? She does not notice the sarcasm in his comment, "So you finished him off, did you, Rita?"

Rita tells Frank that one of the students, Tyson, nicknamed Tiger, has invited her to go to France with a whole group. Frank immediately protests that she cannot go. But he knows that the reason which he gives, her exams, is not the real one. He is jealous and afraid of losing her. Up to now he had been the focal point in her life and had not realised that she would begin to form new relationships. He sees that his influence over her is dwindling. There are whole areas of her life about which he knows nothing. She is becoming a stranger, slipping away from him. Soon she will leave and take all the meaning in his life with her.

When Rita mentions Tiger a second time Frank loses his patience. But Rita's reaction clearly signals that he has gone too far. She is shocked by his suggestion that she is in love with Tiger. Abruptly she breaks off the conversation and asks for his opinion on an essay she has written. When he tells her it would not look out of place with a pile of work done by other, "proper" students she is delighted. Finally she has made it. She is just as well educated as all the others. She does not notice the irony of Frank's remark. The originality and honest responses to literature which once distinguished her from his other students have been buried by conventional, second-hand opinions and so now her essay is no different from all the others.

Act II, Scene 3

Frank has disgraced himself by turning up drunk for one of his lectures. Back in his study he tells Rita what happened. He was apparently so out of control that he fell off the rostrum and now some students have reported him. As he relates the incident we begin to feel that he has sunk to a new level of despair. Perhaps it was the realisation that the old Rita has finally disappeared which made him give up any pretence of taking his teaching seriously. During the lecture he mentioned Rita's definition of assonance, "getting the rhyme wrong". But this dated back to the time when her opinions were all her own. Today she would ridicule her former ignorance and quote a more sophisticated, scholarly definition.

Frank's comment about assonance was a bitter attack on the literary establishment, which takes itself so seriously but, he feels, fails to help people appreciate literature properly. His bitterness is also directed against himself, for he is part of this establishment. The process of educating Rita has shown him even more clearly than before how empty and destructive traditional methods of teaching literature can be.

As soon as Rita sees the state Frank is in she suggests postponing the tutorial. But he insists on discussing an essay she has written on one of Blake's poems. He had expected her to react to it emotionally, without over-complicating it with literary analysis. Instead, she has interpreted it in a very academic way and has obviously taken over other people's opinions, especially those of Trish and some fellow students. When she defiantly asks if her essay is wrong Frank is forced to admit that it would get a good mark in an exam. Its trendiness and sophistication would make it acceptable to most of his colleagues. What he dislikes about it is that her interpretation is second-hand. Once, he thought regretfully, she would have seen the poem for what it is, a simple piece about a flower, described from a child's point of view. The new Rita dissected it with a clinical, analytic eye, searching for symbolism and hidden meaning.

Rita, however, rejects Frank's criticism. She suspects that his pride is hurt because she has not echoed his own ideas. She also accuses him of being unfair because he is criticising the very thing he always wanted her to do, namely to be objective and consult recognised authorities. Ruefully, Frank has to admit that she has a point. He sees how impossible it is to explain his dilemma to her – how to balance the teaching of traditional literary studies with encouraging a true love of literature and honest, personal responses to it. He can only warn her to be careful.

Rita does not understand Frank's warning. He means that whilst consulting the experts she should not let her own reactions be submerged. But she will not allow him to spoil her new-found knowledge, knowledge which has been so hard to acquire. She asserts her independence, accusing him of being over-possessive and telling him she no longer needs his guidance. We begin to wonder whether she even sees herself as his equal. Indeed, there are several signs that their roles are being reversed. Now, for instance, it is Frank rather than Rita who swears. He also takes over her expression "off my cake". Russell seems to be suggesting that they are gradually changing places when Frank sits her down in his own chair. Their reactions to Blake's poem also show that Frank prefers a simple, emotional response, whereas Rita discusses it in the analytic way characteristic of teachers of literature. The idea of role reversal is supported by Frank's enjoyment of the very book, *Rubyfruit Jungle*, which once impressed Rita so much that she changed her name. Condescendingly, she informs him that although it is quite interesting it could never be described as quality literature.

Act II, Scene 4

Rita is late for a tutorial. Her suggestion that they should cancel the session altogether suggests that her lessons are no longer important to her. When she was so late Frank rang the hairdresser's, but was informed that she had not worked there for quite a while. He is hurt and reminds her that she always used to tell him everything. Rita is embarrassed, but also annoyed, resenting this intrusion into her private life. She snaps that she does not want to talk about such a "boring, insignificant detail" as her change of job. One of her reasons for leaving the hairdresser's was that people never talked about anything important, only "irrelevant rubbish". Frank remembers the time when he could hardly get Rita to concentrate on her classes because she was so fascinated by the "boring, insignificant details" of other people's lives – especially his own, he thought ruefully. But apparently the conversation in the bistro where she now works is more interesting. Jealously, Frank asks if Tiger is one of her customers. Rita explains that she enjoys being with the young people in the bistro because they feel strongly about "things that matter" and are "not trapped". Frank does not show how much her comments hurt him. Does she not realise how passionately he feels about the things that matter to him? Yes, he is trapped. He is a poet and does not feel at home in the academic establishment. It is because he is so trapped by his job that he drinks and puts on a cynical, ironic facade. But there is no point in trying to explain all this to Rita. She probably would not be interested.
This was not the first time Rita was late for a tutorial. She has even missed some altogether. Frank suggests that she might want to stop coming. With

his back to her, Rita cannot see the expression on his face. She does not know how important the sessions are to him, how he has come to depend on them. Pathetically, like a discarded lover, he complains that she does not seem to be able to stand his company at all any more. Her reply that she has to attend the tutorials because of her exam cuts him deep. He shows his disappointment by his comment, "I'd rather you spared me that."
Frank is about to pour himself a drink to ease the pain when Rita rebukes him and adds that it is not worth coming to his tutorials because he has nothing important to say. He responds by querying whether she is still capable of recognising what really matters. We are reminded of his warning when he heard that her marriage was breaking up (Act I, scene 5), "When art and literature begin to take the place of life itself, perhaps it's time to ..." (p. 55, ll. 15–16). At the time, Rita chose art and literature in preference to real life because she was trying to escape from a deadening environment. But now art and literature really do seem to be more important than her relationships with other people. She does not answer, but reminds him that she is here to discuss literary criticism. He reacts by asking for her opinion on some of his own poetry.

Act II, Scene 5

Frank is sitting in his study, drinking and listening to the radio. We sense his emptiness and desolation. For a short time Rita had given his teaching career a sense of purpose. He had become increasingly dependent on their classes together, feeding on her vivacity, her honesty and her originality. Now that is all gone. After that brief respite, his life has once more become pointless, but this time with no hope of rescue.
To Frank's astonishment, Rita suddenly walks in. She has read his poems together with her flatmate, Trish. However, Frank is bitterly disappointed when he hears their pompous, pretentious interpretation. Rita was about the only person he thought he could rely on for an honest opinion. His comments are bitterly ironic, but Rita does not notice. Sarcastically, he remarks that he has done a fine job on her and compares himself with Mary Shelley, who wrote *Frankenstein*.
Mary Wollstonecraft Shelley (1797–1851), the wife of the poet Shelley, wrote the novel *Frankenstein* in 1817. It tells the story of how a scientist creates a human being and brings him to life. Lonely and desperate, the creature becomes uncontrollable and the consequences are disastrous. Rita does not understand the implication that Frank, too, has created a monster. By this he means that he has turned her into so much of an expert on literature that she now relies more on borrowed opinions than on her own. This is exactly what Frank had been afraid of. He has made her suppress her emotions and spontaneity.

Finally, Frank asks Rita to go away because he cannot bear her any longer. Misunderstanding him, she is angry. She imagines that he regrets losing his influence over her now that they are on the same level. She accuses Frank and people like him, that is the middle classes, of deliberately keeping the working class down. This reflects Russell's bitter sense of injustice about the fact that the working class are being deprived of a good education and of the chance to participate more fully in cultural life. He feels that they are not being offered the opportunities to make meaningful choices about their lives:

> "Whilst the working-classes are accused of being philistines, there is a general attempt in this country to withhold culture from them [...]. Literature is an invention by the middle-classes for their own benefit. The working-classes haven't accepted literacy yet, which is why it is so difficult teaching working-class kids whose traditions are in the spoken word. That's why I write for the theatre, because it's connected with the spoken rather than the written word." (Charles, 1983, No. 148, pp. 20–21)

Rita tells Frank that she no longer needs him now that she has found a "better culture". When she describes it Frank is surprised. Was that really all she wanted, a room full of books, knowing what clothes to wear, what wine to buy, what plays to see and what papers and books to read? To him that seems very little.

Rita cannot understand why Frank despises everything she has ever coveted. For him getting an education and acquiring culture was so much easier. He took it all for granted, whilst she had to make so many sacrifices. His mockery is like a slap in the face. Angrily she accuses him of squandering his opportunities.

Frank is deeply disappointed. He has tried to educate her, to show her what culture is and now he sees that Rita mistakes the mere attributes of culture for culture itself. Whilst acquiring her education she has lost all the qualities which made her a special person, her spontaneity, her originality, her vitality. Frank uses a metaphor to describe the change in her. In the pub her mother had started crying because she felt they could sing better songs. Now he tells Rita that her "new song" is no better than the old one, but only different and that it sounds shrill, hollow and tuneless. Sadly, he calls her name, wondering if it has all been in vain. But she is blind to his despair and ridicules him for still calling her Rita, the name she rejected as soon as she learned to recognise "good quality" literature. As she leaves, Frank mockingly asks which author she has decided to imitate next, presumably one of quality, such as Virginia (Woolf), Charlotte (Brontë), her sister Emily or Jane (Austen). He is implying that she will exchange one imitation for another because she can no longer be herself.

Act II, Scene 6

Frank and Rita now have so little contact with each other that he has to ring her at work to give her the details of her exam. He does not know, either, that she has reverted to her original name of Susan.

Act II, Scene 7

Frank's surprise at Rita's entrance shows that he had not expected to see her again. It becomes clear that she no longer knows much about his life. He has narrowly escaped being given the sack for drunkenness at work and is going to spend two years in Australia.

Rita has returned to tell Frank that he is a good teacher and to thank him for entering her for the exam. Then she tells him how, sitting in the exam room, she thought about what he had said and realised he was right. She had been so hungry for education and culture that she had accepted the lifestyle and opinions of educated people without a second thought. She had been dazzled by the trappings of culture – books, trendy, fashionable opinions, easy clichés – and had not wanted any of it to be questioned. Now she knows that Frank had not wanted her to stay ignorant, as she had suspected, but had been warning her to remain honest and retain her ability to distinguish between real and imitation.

Russell once described how he himself went through a similar phase to Rita:

> "I overvalued to a ludicrous extent the idea of education, what, you know, college and higher education was and went through a period being very much like Rita, you know, being very bored and suffering from 'art in the head'. I used to stop people and ask them what they thought of Chekhov which was very boring for them. Poor souls on the buses." (Glaap, 1984, p. 95)

Rita has also been affected by Trish's attempted suicide. She had admired her flatmate so much that she had imitated her in everything. The suicide attempt showed her that under Trish's cultured exterior her life was empty and meaningless. Suddenly Rita understands that culture and education do not automatically bring happiness. To lead a fulfilled life she must do more than talk about literature and copy other people's lifestyles. Russell seems to be suggesting that she had simply substituted one mediocre existence for another.

With the exam paper lying in front of her, Rita realised that for the first time in her life she had a real, meaningful choice. She could either give a clever, flippant answer and fail or she could answer in the way the examiners expected. She had come back to thank Frank for giving her that choice.

Rita does not know whether the exam will be of any use to her or not. She has not thought about the next step in her life yet, but that is not important. Gradually Frank begins to recognise the old Rita. Hesitantly, he suggests that she could accompany him to Australia. Her reply is evasive. For one thing, Tiger has invited her to go to France with a group of students. But from her comment about him we suspect that she no longer admires him as she used to. Perhaps she finds him superficial, too. Rita now has several choices, but she has only just begun to take control of her own life and does not want to be pressurised into making any decisions. In an interview Russell explained that it does not really matter what she does next:

> "There's a line in the Paul Simon song *Hearts and Bones*. 'The thought that life could be better is woven indelibly into our hearts and our brains.' It's what my plays are about, the thought that life could be better. I am not interested in how life could be better. I am not interested in whether Rita goes to her mother's, has a baby, finishes her course, or goes to Australia. I am interested that she has got to the point where she can look at those alternatives and feel that she has choice. That for me is the triumph of Rita." (Jones, 1989, p. 335)

Frank gives Rita a present which he once bought for "an educated woman friend". This reminds us of what Rita said at the beginning (scene 2), that she would not buy a new dress until she had passed her first exam. And then it would be a "proper" dress, the type worn by educated women. The dress symbolises her graduation as just such an educated woman. As she accepts it Rita regrets that she has only ever taken things from Frank. He protests, but finds it impossible to explain what she has given him, perhaps a sense of purpose and fulfilment. Suddenly it occurs to her that there is one way she can repay him. He is bewildered, not knowing what to expect. Then, in her old role of Rita, the hairdresser, she pulls out her scissors and starts to cut his hair.

The Characters

Rita

Rita White is an outspoken, down-to-earth young woman from Liverpool's working class. She is twenty-six and so far has always played the role expected by her family, friends and neighbours. Although she is intelligent and has a thirst for learning, at school she rejected educational achievement so that she would not become an outsider. Like her classmates, she focussed instead on pop music, clothes and boys. Now and again it occurred to her that she might be missing something, but she allowed herself to be distracted by new clothes, clubs and boys. Consequently, she left school with hardly any qualifications and trained as a hairdresser. Now, at twenty-six, her husband, Denny, is becoming restless because she has not yet had a baby, like all the other young wives in the neighbourhood.
Suddenly Rita rebels against convention. Without her husband's knowledge she continues to take the pill. She somehow feels that life is passing her by and that there is something missing. She is bored by the superficial conversation of her customers and by endless evenings spent in the pub. The lives of those around her seem narrow and confining. Later on in the play she explains that she sees the working class way of life as a disease, a depressing, day-to-day existence, in which people try to compensate for the poor quality of their lives through consumerism. Rita feels, however, that there is no real cure for their frustration because they have been denied the key to a better quality life, namely a good education. Although Rita rejects their limited horizons and inflexible attitudes, she understands and even feels sorry for them. She also sees that it is this lack of education which prevents her husband from envisaging a better quality of choice than eight different kinds of beer in the local pub.
Eventually Rita becomes so unhappy that she resolves to do something about it. She is aware of her intellectual potential and decides to try to "discover" herself and to find "a better culture". She realises that no one around her will understand her attempt to get to know the "highbrow" kind of culture associated with educated people.
Traditionally the working class reject it as belonging to an alien, elite world, the world of "them", as opposed to their world of "us". Inevitably, her family and friends will feel that she is rejecting them and their norms and values. But Rita is determined to change her life completely. As she herself says, "if you want to change y' have to do it from the inside" (p. 22, ll. 2–3).
Rita's first step in her attempt to catch up on her education and enter a more cultured environment is to enrol for an Open University course in literature.

Her first interview with her tutor, Dr Frank Bryant, reveals her total ignorance of literary studies and of the academic way of thinking in general. The only things in her favour are her lively, original mind, her thirst for learning and her passion for reading. She even changed her name from Susan to Rita because she admired a popular novel written by Rita Mae Brown, *Rubyfruit Jungle*. But her hunger for education is not enough to pass exams. At first she is unable to distinguish between literary works of high quality and popular fiction. To her almost every book is "good" literature. She is also completely ignorant of the methods of literary criticism, thinking that it is sufficient to simply describe her own personal reactions to a book.

Four scenes illustrate Rita's difficulties in learning to appreciate literature from an academic point of view. The first is I,2, in which she rejects E. M. Forster's novel *Howards End* because it is not a true reflection of reality. Her tutor is shocked at such a subjective judgement and tells her that first of all she must learn to be more objective and underpin her views with references to accepted authorities. The next lesson follows in I,3. Acting on Frank's tip that references to other authors impress examiners, Rita has made the mistake of quoting an author of pulp fiction. So now she has to become more selective, which means learning to recognise "quality" literature. She realises that her mind has not been properly trained, "My mind's full of junk, isn't it? It needs a good clearin' out" (p. 44, ll. 14–15).

Rita's lack of training in exam techniques becomes apparent in I,4 when she answers an essay topic in one sentence: she would resolve the difficulties of staging Ibsen's *Peer Gynt* by doing it on the radio. Whilst this illustrates the liveliness and originality of her mind, it also shows that she is not aware of the conventional way of answering examination questions. It is significant that when she takes her exam at the end of the play she is asked the very same question. But by then Rita has learned to play by the academic rules and, perhaps more importantly, she makes a conscious choice to apply them.

Another major step in Rita's education is seeing a stage production of *Macbeth* (I,6). When Frank starts discussing it with her she realises with surprise that academic studies entail more than simply reading or watching works of art. To her the play was no more than an exciting story. She sees that to reach the level of the other, "proper" students she needs to learn a whole new way of thinking. First of all she must acquire the academic code of analysing and interpreting literature. As her studies progress she learns to discipline her mind and think in a more structural, analytical way. Frank sets Rita the task of writing an essay on the play which impressed her so much, *Macbeth*. The work she produces presents him with a dilemma. He finds it moving because it is such an honest, passionate description of her experience. The trouble is, it is too emotional for exam purposes. He has to decide whether he really wants to change her approach to literature. If he forces her to treat it in the more distanced, analytic manner of the academic she might lose her ability to react to it spontaneously and honestly. Rita, however, insists on learning how to write the kind of essay which would get a good mark in an exam. Her ambition is to enter the world of educated people, to find "a better culture" and to do so she must have the passport of a good education. Passing an academic exam becomes a symbol of this better quality life.

Rita's transformation is accompanied by a series of important changes in her personal life. Her marriage breaks up, she moves into a flat with a cultured young woman, gives up her job as a hairdresser to become a waitress in a trendy students' bar and makes new friends among her fellow students. The changes do not come easily. From the outset Rita knew that her quest for a better culture would probably alienate her from her working class background. Although her husband was against her studying she always tried to include him in her new life, inviting him to accompany her to the theatre or, on one occasion, to Frank's house. But he always refused. Gradually, however, the rift between them can no longer be bridged. Rita is aware of Denny's bewilderment as she gradually changes into a different person. In I,5 she tells Frank that sometimes he gives her presents, hoping that they will bring back the old Susan. She understands his accusation that she has in some way betrayed him by rejecting his way of life. But Rita is growing more aware of her own value as a person and is unwilling to surrender any of her newfound independence.

When Rita embarked on the Open University course she knew that she would probably leave her old life behind. She could not wait for the time when she would be able to move freely among the educated middle classes, accepted as one of them. What she could not foresee was that there would be a period somewhere in between when she would be a cultural misfit, alienated from her old culture, but not yet part of a new one. She becomes aware of this when Frank invites her to a dinner party at his house. Standing outside looking through the window, she suddenly realises that she does not belong to his middle class, academic world. The only way she could make his guests accept her would be to entertain them with comical remarks, but that is beneath her dignity. She feels lost in a no-man's-land between one culture and another. As she turns away and reluctantly joins her family in the pub she decides to give up her education and with it her hopes of finding a better culture. Then, in the pub, Rita changes her mind abruptly. She is confronted with her mother's own frustration with her life. This makes her all the more determined not to become trapped by the conventions of her class. Her desire to take control over her own life and to improve the quality of her personal choices is reaffirmed.

Gradually, Rita takes her place among the middle class, socialising with her new flatmate and fellow students. A summer school in London marks her entrance into this new culture. For the first time she finds the self-confidence to speak in front of a lecture-room full of people. As she becomes more knowledgeable and self-assured she begins to feel at home with the other students, even to the point of correcting them when they are wrong. She begins to feel that she has outgrown Frank. She no longer needs his guidance and is so fiercely protective of her new independence that she resents him taking any interest in her private life. This is a very different Rita from the young woman who used to constantly interrupt him with personal questions.

As Rita works her way through the great authors she becomes increasingly familiar with the terminology of literary criticism and is soon able to write the same kind of essays as all the other students. She does not understand Frank's warnings that she should not simply take over other people's opinions, merely because they are educated. He notices, for instance, that she is modelling herself on her new flatmate, Trish. And indeed, through Trish Rita has entered into what she feels is "a better culture". At last she is moving among educated people, people with the "right" books and furniture, who know what kind of wine to buy. One day she even imitates Trish's way of speaking. Frank watches in dismay while she becomes a proficient student, but at the same time loses her refreshing honesty and spontaneity. An essay which she wrote on a poem by William Blake, for instance, is full of sophisticated, trendy opinions, but they are all borrowed. She seems to be afraid of expressing her own feelings in case they are not acceptable. Strangely, Rita and Frank appear to be changing places. Whilst she now approaches literature with the objective, analytic eye of the academic, Frank urges her to appreciate it in a more emotional, subjective way.

After Rita comes back from summer school her relationship with Frank begins to deteriorate. First, she starts criticising him, something she never used to do. On the contrary, she always admired him and envied his education. Now she tries to persuade him to write poetry again and to stop drinking, whereas the old Rita accepted him as he was. Gradually their relationship becomes strained. She no longer attaches so much importance to their tutorials, at times coming late and sometimes not turning up at all. She hardly shows any interest in his private life and does not inform him about changes in her own, such as her new flatmate, her change of job or the fact that she now calls herself Susan again. At one time he was the most important person in her life, always the first to know about any important new experience, such as the performance of *Macbeth*. When he challenges her about this she turns on him in anger, saying that such things are only boring, minor details and that she prefers to discuss more interesting subjects. Apparently she is referring to the type of conversations she holds with students in the bar where she works. She describes these new friends as people who are "not trapped" (p. 100, l. 19). This is reminiscent of Rita's former life, when she felt imprisoned by the limitations and prejudices of her working class environment. She now seems to feel that she has escaped to a world in which people are free of such social pressures.

The tension between them eventually explodes in II,5. Frank had asked for Rita's opinion on some of his poems, which in itself is a reversal of their former roles. He is bitterly disappointed when she gives him sophisticated, second-hand opinions instead of her own personal reactions. He has to recognise that his worst fears have come true. The old Rita with her passionate, honest responses to literature, has completely disappeared. Sarcastically, he suggests that a monster has taken her place, a monster who is so blinded by her new "culture" that she can no longer form judgements of her own. He accuses her of being unable to tell what really matters in life, unable to distinguish what is real from imitation.

Then, suddenly, Rita's life takes a different turn again. Trish, the cultured woman she admires so much, has tried to kill herself. Shocked, Rita realises that her flatmate's sophisticated manners, her good taste and clever opinions on art and literature, were nothing but a shiny veneer, with no real substance behind it. She understands now that Frank is right. He had stood by and watched whilst she copied Trish and all the other so-called educated people around her. He had tried to warn her not to lose herself by copying others, but she had not listened. Once she had even accused him of deliberately trying to prevent her from reaching the same level as himself so that he could still look down on her. But she had been wrong. He really had been concerned about her. After taking her exam she goes back to thank him for everything and to admit that he had been right. She had indeed mistaken the appearance of culture for real education. Trish's attempted suicide makes it clear to her that there is more to life than art and literature.

By the end of the play Rita sees clearly what had happened to her. She had escaped from the confining attitudes of her original environment only to exchange one set of conventions for another. She had blindly taken over the accepted, orthodox opinions of so-called experts. Instead of an education, she had merely gained knowledge. But now, finally, she has acquired the freedom she was seeking without losing her personality. She has been trained to think in a more structured, analytical way and is able to make more informed choices. If she decides not to watch ballet or opera on TV it will be because she chooses not to and not from sheer prejudice.

Rita also has wider, more meaningful choices of what to do with her life. There are several immediate possibilities, for instance she could accompany Frank to Australia, go on holiday in France with a group of students or even spend Christmas with her parents. This last alternative shows that she has achieved a balance between her old self and the new. Knowing she now has the choice of whether to conform to the conventions of her old environment or not, she is able to contemplate the possibility of spending Christmas there. Russell himself makes the following comment about Rita's transformation:

> "At the end of the play what I'm trying to show is somebody who synthesizes the best of what she can gain from literature and what she can get from *Rubyfruit Jungle* [...]. One's talking about a complex woman. It's also, of course, something to do with class. I'm talking about somebody who synthesizes the best of two classes and trying to attack the divisions really in teaching, in education, and in the class system. And so it's the division and it's the elitist way in which literature is dealt with that I really object to." (Glaap, 1984, p. 22)

This balance between the old and the new, between Rita and Susan, the hairdresser and the student, is illustrated by her act of cutting Frank's hair in the last scene. She has come full circle, slipping back into the role of hairdresser, but with the all-important difference that she can now choose whether or not to work as a hairdresser.

Frank

The first impression of Dr Frank Bryant, Rita's university tutor, does not inspire confidence. He obviously has a drinking problem. But we also learn from a phone conversation that he is witty, with a taste for irony and even sarcasm. Nevertheless, he represents a different culture and is Rita's key to a better way of life.

Frank did not aspire to being a university lecturer. In fact, he is really a poet. However, since he could not make a living from it he turned to lecturing in English literature. Over the years he has grown bored and frustrated and now, in his early fifties, he is disillusioned and cynical. Later, when Rita knows him better, she comments on his cynicism, suggesting that he hides his feelings behind this facade. And indeed, as the play progresses, we begin to understand that he is actually a very sensitive person, but has perhaps been so deeply hurt in the past that he now feels the need to protect himself.

Frank is frustrated with his work because he loves literature, but recognises that for the majority of his students a university degree is no more than a passport to a relatively affluent, secure future. And those who do show an interest in the subject soon learn which responses are expected. The essays which they hand in are full of conventional interpretations, supported by acceptable quotations from established literary authorities.

Frank's frustration extends to the whole of the literary establishment. He hates the smugness and pretentiousness of the so-called experts. At one point Frank explains to Rita that as a poet he made the mistake of trying to write "literature", or the sort of work which would be acceptable to literary critics and could be studied and "appreciated" by students. These days he no longer thinks he has anything important to say and has stopped writing poetry altogether. Today Frank feels that all he is really required to do is to relay traditional, conventional opinions on established authors to mediocre students so that they can pass exams. The only way he can face this task is with the help of alcohol. Drinking also helps him to forget or suppress his frustration in other areas of his life. He has split up from his wife and is now living with a former student called Julia, but his bitter remarks about both women suggest that he has also been very disappointed in his private life.

Then, suddenly, Frank is confronted with someone with a genuine love of literature and a burning desire to learn. He immediately realises that this young hairdresser has a far greater thirst for learning than the average student. As their first meeting progresses he begins to recognise that Rita is indeed quite unique. Although her mind is completely untrained and she has absolutely no idea about literature, she is highly intelligent and also very honest. Her total ignorance of literary studies means that for the first time in his teaching career a student is not afraid to give him her spontaneous, emotional reactions to literature. This, together with her originality and wit, makes him feel as if she is the first breath of fresh air which has been in his room for years. He is fascinated by her enthusiasm, unpredictability, energy and her independent mind.

Yet Frank does not leap at the chance to teach Rita. After she has explained her reasons for taking the course he realises just how much it means to her. He suspects that this will force him to examine his own assumptions more closely and he is not sure whether he really wants his rather boring, but comfortable existence to be disturbed to such an extent. He is probably also afraid of being unable to fulfil Rita's demands.

Nevertheless, against his better judgement, Frank decides to accept his new student. It is as he feared. Her complete ignorance about literature and traditional methods of literary studies force him to explain and justify even the most basic concepts. He is often confused and embarrassed when she asks him to explain things which he had never really questioned, such as the difference between light reading and "good" literature. Frank is aware that Rita with her untutored mind is capable of responding to literature in a much more direct, honest way than most of his students and colleagues. Through Rita Russell is challenging the esoteric attitudes of traditional university studies by forcing Frank to question his own understanding of his work and of himself. (For more details see Theme 4).

At various times throughout the play, Frank tries to explain why he does not really want to teach her. He is afraid that once she has learned the conventional methods of approaching literature she will suppress her refreshing spontaneity and honesty in order to pass exams. Worst of all, he himself would be responsible for any such change. But since she refuses to go to any other tutor he has to find a way of helping her to acquire the "better culture" which she so desperately desires without destroying her uniqueness. Knowing how much her studies mean to her, it is impossible to refuse.

No matter how much Rita tells Frank about her background, he cannot really understand what she is up against. He does not seem to have had any contact at all with working class people. At most he may have a romanticised view of their way of life, based on what he has read in novels. Even after Rita has painted a depressing picture of working class culture he cannot see anything wrong with it as long as people believe they are happy. Unlike Rita, Frank does not think in political terms. Although he follows her argument about the link between poor education and limited choices, he does not really understand what this means to the people involved. Nor is he very interested. He is not as much aware of social class as Rita. Throughout the play she makes references to the differences between the classes. Indeed, her whole aim is to escape into a better educated social class.

Frank's insensitivity to Rita's position is also demonstrated when he invites her and her husband, Denny, to a dinner party at his house. It obviously does not occur to him that he is putting Rita in a very embarrassing position. Apart from the conflict it might cause between the couple, he does not consider how uncomfortable they would feel among his academic friends. When Rita does not turn up Frank reproaches her for upsetting the arrangements, but we suspect that really he was very disappointed. Rita is too ignorant of middle class academic culture to know that in his circles Frank, too, is an outsider. He despises this "better culture" of which he is a part, the one Rita aspires to. He probably only found the thought of the dinner party bearable because of the prospect of Rita's company.

Typical middle class housing for people like Frank

Rita has to spell out to him why she could not come. His lack of understanding once again shows that he is completely unaware of the difficulties facing people from her background. He is totally unsympathetic, first suggesting that she should see a psychiatrist, then asking why she does not simply give the course up if it is causing so many problems. He is unaware of all the sacrifices Rita has made and does not see that it is now impossible for her to revert to her former life. It is only when Denny throws her out that he finally begins to grasp just how much she has become alienated from her original environment.

Despite his continuing reservations, Frank perseveres in equipping Rita to pass exams. Eventually he has to admit that her work is no different from that of his other students. Rita is delighted and does not notice the irony in his remark. Sadly, Frank sees that his worst fears have been realised and that she now writes the standard type of essay which examiners expect. Her responses are no longer her own, but second-hand, no longer emotional and original, but controlled, analytical and full of references to accepted authorities.

As Rita becomes more proficient she grows away from Frank. He notices that she begins to develop other relationships and that he is not the most important person in her life any more. He is hurt that her classes mean so little to her that she sometimes arrives late or not at all. He also notices that she no longer informs him of changes in her private life, as she used to. When he tackles her about this she is offended, feeling that he is intruding. He is also hurt by her comment that she prefers to be with people who are "not trapped". Rita does not realise that he himself feels trapped. He is really a poet and does not fit into established academic life. It is partly this sense of failure which has made him turn to drink. But Rita does not understand this and, he feels, would no longer be interested. He sees that she is slipping away from him and becoming a stranger. Gradually, he begins to dislike the person she is changing into. At one point he even says he will be glad when she leaves. But Rita is blind to his despair at having lost the one person who had given his teaching some sense of purpose. He had looked forward to their tutorials and had even become dependent on them to brighten up his existence.

Frank's disappointment is acute when Rita returns from a summer school in London. He can cope with her changed appearance and attempts to influence him, trying to make him stop drinking and write poetry again. But he is devastated when she tells him she has already read the poems of William Blake. He had been saving them up to read with her. They mean a lot to him and he had been looking forward to seeing her reactions and to guiding her towards a better understanding of them. He is even more disappointed with the essay which she writes on Blake. Instead of expressing her own feelings she describes the poems in the sophisticated, but second-hand jargon of literary criticism. Frank feels betrayed. He was counting on what he thought was

Rita's unspoiled mind to see Blake the way he does, emotionally and without over-complicating him.

Later, when Frank asks for Rita's opinion on his own poems, her reaction makes it clear to him that the person he knew and liked has completely disappeared, probably forever. As before, her views are not her own, but borrowed. Frank is in despair. He had asked for her thoughts in a last attempt to save their relationship, to bind her closer to him. Also, she is the only person he knows who will give him an honest opinion, or so he had thought. Angry and bitter, he tells her that he has created a monster. He has turned her into so much of an expert on literature that she now relies more on conventional, second-hand opinions than on her own. This is exactly what he was afraid would happen. He has been instrumental in making her suppress her originality and her emotions. He is so disappointed that he can no longer stand the sight of her.

Frank's request for Rita's opinions on his poems reverses their normal positions, for suddenly the student is supposed to judge the teacher. In fact, there are times when Frank very much resembles the old Rita, for instance in his request for a simple, emotional response to Blake's poems. Rita, on the other hand, prefers the kind of impersonal, objective analysis which he used to demand from her. Another aspect of this role reversal is Frank's new interest in Rita's private life. In the earlier stages of their relationship she was the one who asked the personal questions. These days, however, the only thing she wants to discuss with him is literature.

The growing tension between Frank and Rita comes to a head when he expresses contempt for her newly acquired culture. To him, knowing which books to read and having the "right" furniture does not constitute being educated. On the contrary, he despises most of the so-called "cultured" people around him. He particularly finds the way his cultured colleagues teach and expect him to teach literature soulless and limiting, as proved by Rita's development. For him education is more than the transmission of knowledge, skills and exam techniques. He tries to develop a person's whole being, appealing to the heart as well as the head.

At the beginning of the play Frank explained one of his teaching principles to Rita, that of allowing learners to find things out for themselves. He tries to achieve a balance between teaching the accepted code of literary studies and helping his students to become more sensitive and aware.

Besides allowing students to develop and discover things for themselves it is also a point in Frank's favour that, although he disliked what Rita was asking him to do, he respected her wishes.

After the quarrel in which Frank questioned the value of Rita's new-found culture they lose touch with each other for a while. They actually become so estranged that Frank does not even know that Rita has reverted to her old name of Susan. Having lost the one person who gave him some sense of pur-

pose in life, he falls into an even deeper despair than before. Never again will he experience the same sense of purpose and fulfilment as he did with this eager young hairdresser. Under Rita's influence he had cut down on alcohol, but now there is no reason to control himself. One day he turns up drunk at a lecture, with the result that his superiors suggest a two year sabbatical in Australia.
As Frank is packing to leave the country, Rita comes in. She has taken her exam and wants to thank him for everything. She also admits that he had been right. She had been so enthusiastic about her new knowledge and skills that she had lost sight of herself. As she talks Frank recognises the old Rita re-emerging. They are now on the same level. There is not much more he can teach her about literature, so the dependence of the student on the teacher has disappeared. In fact, if anything it is Rita who is now the more dominant figure. Since they have found their way back to their old relationship Frank sees no reason why he should not invite her to accompany him to Australia. But Rita is just beginning to enjoy her independence and does not want to be pressed into making any decisions about her future yet. Typically, Frank does not insist, but allows her time to make up her own mind. The ending is left open. She might join him in Australia, but then again she might not. The last scene is a reminder of where Rita stood at the beginning of her studies. Once more she slips into her role of hairdresser as she prepares to "take ten years off" him by cutting his hair. When asked about this ending Russell said that it was not intended to be anything more than a humorous gag. But literary students might defy him and interpret it as a symbol of the beginning of Frank's rejuvenation.

Denny/Rita's Mother/Trish

Denny, Rita's mother and Trish are important because of their dramatic function in the play rather than for their individual characteristics.

Denny

Rita's husband Denny (short for Dennis) represents the inflexible attitudes and limited horizons which Rita finds so constraining. He has been brought up to believe that the man is the head of the household and that his wife should obey him. He cannot understand Rita's needs at all. She tries to explain and even attempts to involve him by inviting him to accompany her to the theatre. She also compromises by doing her studying at work in order to avoid arguments. But Denny stubbornly refuses to listen. Eventually he issues an ultimatum. She must either live with him on his terms, which means giving up her studies, or not at all.

Besides his function as a representative of the repressive culture from which Rita wants to escape, Denny's personality also forms a sharp contrast to Rita's. He is not a deep thinker and cannot understand what she means by a different quality of choice. He does not really see women as having much choice anyway. For him their only role in life is to become wives and mothers. Rita's rebellion completely baffles him. His world is one in which nothing ever changes. He is completely at home in an environment where choice is defined as eight different kinds of beer in the local pub. In this respect, too, he represents the kind of limited, inflexible mentality which Rita hates. At one point she explains to Frank that people from her background exert tremendous pressure on each other to conform. She feels that this is because they are afraid of change. Anyone who tries to break out is perceived as a threat and made to feel an outsider. Denny illustrates this kind of attitude by his refusal to try to understand his wife's needs. When it becomes clear that she will not revert to her former self, but is determined to alter her life, he rejects her. His refusal to contemplate any kind of change is stronger than the need to keep his wife. His attitude to change is expressed in his accusation that Rita has "betrayed" him, meaning that by turning away from the traditional working class way of life she is also rejecting his norms and values.
Denny's reluctance to face up to problems is illustrated by the scene in the pub where Rita's mother starts to cry for no apparent reason. Instead of trying to find out what is wrong Denny cheers her up again. He probably realises what she is thinking, but refuses to allow anything to disturb the framework of traditional values on which he has built his life. At one point Rita explains to Frank that her husband is not so unintelligent that he would not be able to understand her, it is rather that "he's blind, he doesn't want to see" (p. 23, l. 17). The contrast with Denny's need for the security of traditional norms makes Rita's decision to break away seem all the more courageous.

Rita's Mother

Rita's mother is important because she leads the kind of life her daughter would have if she accepted the traditional role of women. It is Mrs White's disappointment and frustration that makes Rita even more determined to avoid falling into the same trap herself.

Trish

Trish (short for Patricia) is only briefly mentioned, but it is obvious that Rita models herself on her flatmate, taking over her opinions and even, for a while, her way of speaking. Rita sees Trish as an embodiment of the "better culture" which she herself is so desperately seeking. However, Trish's attempted suicide shows Rita that her flatmate's world is really very empty and that underneath the cultured exterior Trish's life is shallow and meaningless. Her suicide attempt makes Rita see that she herself had only exchanged one set of meaningless choices for another. She had been taken in by appearances such as the "right" books on the shelves and by clever-sounding opinions. Trish's attempt to kill herself is the catalyst which makes Rita stop and think. From then on she is able to distinguish between real education and pretentiousness.

Themes

1. Cultural Divisions between the Social Classes in Britain

Russell is very conscious of the differences between the social classes in Britain. Like Rita, he, too, was brought up in a working class family and left school early with very few qualifications. His reasons for taking up his education at a later stage were similar to Rita's, he "wanted to know" what he had missed. He feels very strongly that education reinforces the division between the social classes and that the working class is at a great disadvantage. (For more details see Themes 2 and 3).

Whilst being aware of differences in middle and working class cultures, Russell finds it difficult to define them. He actually denies that there is any such thing as a specifically "working class culture", suggesting instead that it is a mixture:

> "But is there a pure working-class culture? No, I don't think of it as pure because it's a hybrid culture really [...]. I am aware of, without really being able to define it, the difference between a high art culture and what we, for the sake of convenience, call a working-class culture. And it's easier to define a high art culture than it is to describe the hybrid, working-class culture." (Jones, 1989, pp. 320–321)

There is, however, one point on which he is clear:

> "I don't believe that you can give the working-class a middle-class culture, because a working-class culture is still based upon the word spoken and not the word written. It's still an oral-based culture and not a literary culture. A middle-class culture is a literary culture; information is carried in the written word. Still today in the working-classes the information and the code is dealt with in the spoken word and that's why it's terribly difficult to teach working-class kids, because teaching is a middle-class process: it's conducted by the middle-classes with reference to literature ninety-nine percent of the time." (Glaap, 1984, pp. 28–29)

Unlike some other playwrights and sociologists, Russell does not romanticise about the working class. Instead, he attacks the inflexibility which causes them to reject things which are not part of their traditions. He criticises the bigoted, conservative aspects of working class life which prevent individuals from developing. The theme of a working class person fighting to escape from a repressive family and community runs through his plays.

Attempts have been made to describe the cultural differences between the social classes. Longman's *Dictionary of English Language and Culture* (1992, p. 1258) suggests the following categories:

- *Food:* The British middle classes are more likely to eat healthily and to try foreign food than the working class. This point comes out in Russell's play when Rita labels Frank as a "Flora man" who eats "pebble-dashed bread", meaning that he is health-conscious. Frank also mentions that his girlfriend often prepares the French dish ratatouille. This would be very unusual in a working class home, where more traditional food would be served. It is also relatively rare for working class people to visit restaurants.
- *Education:* Given the choice, the middle classes would prefer to send their children to either public or grammar schools rather than comprehensives. They also encourage them to go on to college or university. Working class children almost always attend comprehensives and if they continue with their education after school-leaving age it will probably be at a college of technology or of education.
- *Work / jobs:* Whereas young middle class people often go into professions such as teaching, medicine or finance, their working class equivalents do less qualified work, for instance as hairdressers, mechanics, shop assistants or lorry drivers.
- *Housing:* Home ownership is higher among the middle classes. They tend to live in detached or semi-detached houses in the suburbs, as does Frank. The working class, on the other hand, often rent council houses or flats and often live in the inner cities, like Rita.
- *Leisure:* It is the middle class rather than the working class which enjoys the products of "high culture", such as the theatre, museums and art galleries. Rita's suggestion that Frank watches BBC television rather than ITV is also substantiated by reality. Generally speaking, the middle class prefers the more serious programmes on BBC 2 and Channel 4 rather than the lighter entertainment on ITV. *Educating Rita* illustrates another difference in leisure activities. Dinner parties, such as Frank's, are never given by the working class. They prefer to meet in pubs, like Rita's family, and working men's clubs. This explains Rita's ignorance about which wine to take to Frank's. Wine bars are usually preferred by the middle classes.
- *Sports and games:* Middle class sports tend to be cricket, golf, tennis, skiing and sailing, as opposed to the working class preferences for football, darts, horse racing, bingo, snooker and, in the north, racing pigeons.
- *Politics:* Traditionally the middle classes are associated with the Conservative and Liberal parties, whereas the working class have usually voted Labour, at least for the "Old" Labour Party. These cultural differences are still highly important, especially in England. They have been described as "the unseen skeletal structure of England" (*The Spectator*, 13 March 1993, p. 10). Whenever two English people meet they immediately try to place

> each other in the social hierarchy. Giving the right signals makes the difference between being accepted as one of the in-group, "us", or rejected as one of "them". Consider the following description of such cultural differences: "the under-landscape of English life, the uninspected networks of admission and exclusion – that is the really significant thing [...] it relies on tiny little signals of acceptability and training of not-quite-rightness and not quite-usness" (*The Spectator*, p. 9; usness = "us"-ness).

Since the end of the 1970s, when Russell's play is set, the social class system in England has changed considerably. The traditional working class represented by Rita, her mother and husband has been drastically reduced in numbers. With the decline of the manufacturing industry many manual jobs were lost and trade union membership declined. The growth of light industries and services and better educational opportunities has led to a "new working class" which has adopted the habits and lifestyles of the lower middle class. At the same time a new "underclass" has developed, consisting of the unemployed, the poor, the elderly, the homeless, ethnic minorities and single-parent families. All these groups are often completely dependent on state benefits. For further details see Detlef & Margaret von Ziegésar, *Grundwissen. Landeskunde United Kingdom*, Stuttgart: Klett, 2000, ch. 8: "Social Structure".

2. Social Class and Education

The value of education for personal development is a thread which runs through Russell's work. Although *Educating Rita* does not have an overt political message, it certainly implies that education can be used as a tool for emancipating working class individuals. The immense popularity of the play indicates that audiences understand Rita's point of view. Some may even feel encouraged to follow her example. For Rita's progress illustrates that education is more than gaining access to a better job and a higher social class. It is also the means by which people can recognise and develop their own potential.

As Rita turns into an educated member of the middle class she leaves her working class environment behind. The question arises as to whether she was right to persevere with something which alienated her from her own kind. Russell himself answers this question: "with English class structure the way it is Rita has to be better off for having taken her course of action" (*The Times Higher Educational Supplement*, 4 July 1980).

In an interview Russell once claimed that in Britain education is a social divider. His belief is still valid today. Rita is an example of one of the masses of young working class people who leave school with hardly any qualifications. In contrast, those whose parents can afford public schools are almost automatically destined to join the social elite. Unemployment is virtually unknown, for instance, among former students of Eton public school. In 1993 the headmaster estimated that the figure was no higher than four percent and that, even more significantly, it had not risen over the previous five years. At that time sixteen of the top hundred jobs in the City were held by old Etonians (cf. *The Spectator*, 13 March 1993, p. 10).

3. Education, "High Culture" and "Low Culture"

Whilst Russell's play propagates education as a means of emancipation, at the same time it highlights the dangers of passing on norms and values without reflection. Education is presented as a potentially liberating, but also limiting process if students' opinions are standardised. Through *Educating Rita* Russell, who was once a teacher himself, examines the question of the academic study of literature and expresses his doubts about traditional teaching methods. Frank's consistent attempts to dampen Rita's enthusiasm for the literary theories which she picks up give voice to Russell's fears that a spontaneous love of art can easily be suppressed by traditional interpretation methods and exam techniques. Frank does not want Rita to become so dependent on established literary criticism that she is afraid of expressing her own ideas, especially if they are unconventional.

Towards the end of the play Rita accuses Frank of taking his own education for granted. Indeed, Russell does seem to be suggesting that Frank lacks sympathy and understanding for people in Rita's position. The wider implication is that educated members of the middle class, like Frank, know almost nothing about the lives of those less privileged than themselves and, furthermore, do not care.

Through the figure of Frank, Russell expounds his belief that literary critics and traditional approaches to literature are partly responsible for the cultural division between the social classes. For Frank is part of what Russell calls the "literature industry", composed of those who define, evaluate and teach literature:

> "There's something I call the 'literature industry' which has sprung up and which I particularly loathe because it seems to me to put a huge barrier between the Ritas of this world who want to learn and literature itself. It probably comes out in my own sort of situation; for years and years and years I wouldn't pick a classical or known and regarded author from the bookshelves. I'd rather read a racy, accessible American novel or indeed quality American novels because they were rarely classified as literature [...]. [I'm] trying to attack the divisions really in teaching, in education, and in the class system. And so it's the division and it's the elitist way in which literature is dealt with that I really object to." (Glaap, 1984, p. 21)

Russell sees this "literature industry" as part of a broader "high art culture", which also incorporates other types of art. He attacks this industry for suggesting, firstly, that there is such a thing as "high culture", secondly for deciding what belongs in this category and, lastly, for spreading the idea that these cultural products are only intended for a very well educated minority:

> "High art is refined art – opera houses, poetry books, concert halls, theatres. Just as I don't want the class division, I really don't want those cultural divisions. I want the concert hall, and the opera stage, and the poetry book to mean just as much to Joe as they do to Joseph [...]. How you ever achieve that, I don't know, but it would be better if you didn't have a high art culture and a polarized working-class culture [...]. We do have a literature industry, an opera industry, a theatre industry, and the spokesmen are generally people who think that art is only for the few [...]. The shapers, the makers, of the stranglehold are the writers *about* it, the communicators about it, not the communicators themselves. I know for example when first I wanted to write drama, I diligently read *Theatre Quarterly* and *Drama Magazine*. I could feel all the time being pulled into one approved direction, one approved style. There was a Michael Radcliffe piece in *The Observer* that presents us with what he thinks we should go and see. And he wants us to be guilty about going to see what we do see." (Jones, 1989, pp. 321–322)

Russell argues that the working class has no access to that part of Britain's culture which is normally described as "high" or "highbrow". This is partly due to their own attitudes. Rita explains to Frank that people from her class normally reject the "higher" forms of art, such as ballet and opera, without even trying to understand them. They feel that such things are reserved for the better educated middle classes, whilst they themselves prefer the more easily accessible, "lowbrow" products of the popular or mass-mediated culture. But besides criticising the attitudes of the working class themselves, Russell also blames the elitist way highbrow culture is presented to them. In an attempt to improve this situation he decided to write plays specifically for working class audiences:

> "Whilst the working-classes are accused of being philistines, there is a general attempt in this country to withhold culture from them [...]. Literature is an invention by the middle-classes for their own benefit. The working-classes haven't accepted literacy yet, which is why it is so difficult teaching working-class kids whose traditions are in the spoken word. That's why I write for the theatre, because it's connected with the spoken rather than the written word." (Charles, 1983, pp. 20–21)

Russell's questioning of traditional definitions of "high culture" is expressed particularly through the clash of Rita's and Frank's backgrounds in the first scene. To Rita best-sellers and classical authors are all literature of equal standing, all "books". When she asks Frank to explain the difference he is embarrassed, realising that he has never really thought about traditional notions of what exactly constitutes quality literature. The scene makes the audience aware that the definitions of some cultural products as "highbrow" and others as "light entertainment" are rather arbitrary. In fact, no such dividing line existed before about the middle of the nineteenth century. In 1834 some laws were passed which split drama theatres from music halls and other popular places of entertainment. The term *legitimate* was then used to refer to "high culture" or drama, and *non-legitimate* for variety shows and cabaret. From this time on the working class were made to feel that the more popular types of entertainment were less valuable than other art forms. Since that time there has been a continuing discussion about which cultural forms are more important than others. The categories for defining them have also shifted over the years. This process is particularly well illustrated in the cinema. For instance, the early Chaplin films were once regarded as popular entertainment, but today they enjoy the status of classics.

4. Education and the Meaning of Life

What education means to Rita

Rita wants to acquire an education in order to give her life more meaning and to "discover herself". Through education she hopes to become a different person, someone who is more "real". As she tries to acquire an education the following philosophical questions are raised:
- What does education actually mean?
- Can education be equated with a meaningful life, the "real life" which Rita is searching for? Is the life of her highly educated teacher, Frank, for instance, more "real" than her own?
- Can education help Rita to "discover herself"? What is a person's true self?

What education means to Frank

The play contrasts Rita's and Frank's ideas of education. Whereas Rita puts all her hopes for a better life into education, Frank no longer has any aims or ideals at all. He is disillusioned with formal education and hates the whole literary and educational establishment, although he loves literature itself. He distinguishes between "poetry" and "literature", explaining, "Instead of creating poetry I spent – oh – years and years trying to create literature" (p. 58, ll. 2–4). By this he means that rather than simply writing what he felt he tried to produce something which the literary establishment would approve of. He detests the academic approach to literature because students are trained to suppress their emotional responses to it.

Once Frank has agreed to take Rita on he proves to be a very good teacher. He realises that he is faced with an enormous challenge for not only does he have to teach her the techniques of literary criticism, but also a completely new, analytic way of thinking. One instance illustrates Frank's qualities as a teacher. After struggling with the novel *Howards End*, Rita finally comes to understand Forster's phrase "only connect". When she asks Frank why he hadn't simply explained it to her, saving her a lot of time and trouble, he explains, "you'll have a much better understanding of something if you discover it in your own terms" (p. 52, ll. 5–7).

While Rita learns the accepted techniques of literary criticism Frank watches in despair as her fresh, original response to literature is replaced by the objective kind of analysis which will enable her to pass exams. Her opinions are no longer her own, but are shaped by literary critics. The more proficient she becomes the more he hates himself as the instrument of this destruction. Did he not tell her, "try to remember that criticism is purely objective. [...] In criticism sentiment has no place" (p. 33, ll. 7–12)?

Frank is horrified at the changes in Rita when she returns from summer school for she has become self-confident to the point of arrogance. He is shocked, too, that she mistakes symbols of "culture" for a true education. She tells him, "I've got a room full of books. I know what clothes to wear, what wine to buy, what plays to see, what papers and books to read" (p. 105, ll. 18–20). Frank scorns her for being so easily satisfied, "Is that all you wanted. Have you come all this way for so very, very little?" (p. 105, ll. 22–23). He is disappointed and disgusted because Rita seems to be defining education in terms of increased social prestige. Her behaviour when she returns from summer school shows him that she is moving further and further away from her original goal of creating a more meaningful life for herself.

The depths of Frank's despair reveal how passionately he actually feels about education – not formal education, but the kind which involves the whole of the personality, including emotions. To him one essential element of a "real" education is to develop a critical awareness of the world in general. His remark "Everything I know [...] is that I know absolutely nothing" (p. 25, ll. 10–12) echoes Socrates' "I know that I do not know". It is a warning that nothing should be taken for granted, all basic assumptions should be questioned. Frank's critical attitude toward his academic environment illustrates the questioning attitude of those who are humble enough to understand how little they really know about the world. His academic colleagues, on the other hand, are so self-satisfied that they do not doubt their own status as "experts", nor do they questions basic assumptions, for instance about the nature of "literature" and "culture".

Frank's concept of education is one which values wonder and delight at everything the world has to offer, but also doubt and constant questioning. This is not only negative and destructive, for without reflection and questioning there would be no progress, society would stand still.

What has education done for Rita at the end

Frank sees his task as giving Rita a "real" education in the wider sense of making her more conscious of the world around her and enabling her to make informed decisions as opposed to irrational ones based on ignorance and prejudice. Because she has had so little formal education she will not be able to think about much at all until she has acquired more knowledge and skills. So first he has to give her some basic tools – a familiarity with certain works of art, the ability to form judgements on the basis of reasoned thought and the skill of expressing herself clearly and in the accepted language of the academic world.

Before long Rita is on the same level as the other students. Besides new knowledge and skills she has also gained self-confidence, a new lifestyle and a new circle of friends. She feels there is nothing more for Frank to teach her, "I've got what you have [...]. I don't need you" (p. 105, ll. 12, 16). But Rita mistakes the symbols of culture for real education. It is only when her cultured, educated flatmate Trish tries to commit suicide that she understands the limitations of a formal education. She realises that her expectations of education were unrealistic and that education in itself does not automatically guarantee a more meaningful life.

Education does, however, open up more possibilities. By getting to know a different way of life and learning to think in a new way Rita has managed to distance herself from a world of conventional expectations and limited choices. At the end she understands and appreciates Frank's belief that formal education has its limitations and that true education means liberation from the constraints of fixed thought patterns. She thanks him for liberating her by giving her the means to achieve more personal freedom, the freedom to make decisions based on knowledge and critical reflection, "Because of what you'd given me I had a choice" (p. 109, l. 28 f.). Finally she has found the answer to her initial question, "God, what's it like to be free?" (p. 15, l. 6).

5. False Appearances

The theme of false appearances runs through the whole play, underlining Russell's message about the discrepancy between formal and "true" education.

Frank

Frank himself illustrates the fact that an academic education in itself is no guarantee of happiness. His knowledge, abilities and social position are no more than a facade covering up the emptiness of his life.
A second reading of the play makes us aware of the significance of his hiding the bottles behind the books. This is the first suggestion that all is not well behind the scenes. The hidden bottles comically reinforce Frank's conviction that academic expertise about literature can be used as a veneer of culture and social prestige. Frank himself makes use of this facade to hide his frustration with everyday life, with his lack of success as a poet and with the way he is forced to teach literature at university. The idea of false pretences is also echoed in his relationship with his employers, who know about his drinking but are prepared to tolerate it as long as he keeps up appearances.

Rita

At the beginning of the play Susan has changed her name to Rita, because she admired a book written by someone with that name. A warning note is sounded when she criticises her customers for believing that a change of hairstyles makes them into different people, "they come to the hairdresser's cos they wanna be changed. But if you want to change y' have to do it from the inside" (p. 22, ll. 1–3). Susan's change of name eventually proves just as superficial as her customers' new hairstyles. It is the first step in her construction of an educated, cultured facade.
The changes of name chart Rita's progress. When she learns that the author she admired so much writes so-called "pulp" or "inferior" fiction, she is ashamed of the name and reverts to Susan, telling Frank, "Nobody calls me Rita but you. I dropped that pretentious crap as soon as I saw it for what it was" (p. 106, ll. 3–5). She finds the name Susan more suitable for what she believes is her more cultured environment.
The theme of false pretences is taken up again when Rita returns from summer school. Outward signs of changes in her personality are a different style of dressing, "second-hand clothes" (p. 77, l. 7), and a new set of friends. Gradually, with the help of her new flatmate, Trish, Rita acquires more and more symbols of an educated, cultured individual – the "right" tastes in clothes, books, films and food.

Trish replaces Frank as a role model and Rita unquestioningly copies everything she says and does. To Rita, Trish personifies what she herself has been looking for – more and better choices in life and the freedom to decide for herself what kind of life to lead. It is only when Trish tries to commit suicide that her sophisticated exterior is revealed as a false pretence. Like Frank, Trish tried to hide inner emptiness and frustration behind a veneer of education and culture. The destruction of Trish's facade makes Rita recognise that the kind of choices which Trish had were superficial and that a "true" education goes much deeper.

Denny

Denny, too, illustrates the theme of false pretences. Instead of trying to understand his wife's problems he prefers to ignore them. Rita explains to Frank, "he doesn't want to see" (p. 23, l. 17). Similarly, when his mother-in-law bursts into tears in the pub Denny does not try to find out what is wrong, but tries to cheer her up, "Ten minutes later, Denny had her laughing [...] pretending she hadn't said it" (p. 72, ll. 19–20). It is this inflexibility and refusal to face up to problems that eventually drives Rita away from him.

6. Gender Roles

General Information

Sex and gender differences

Educating Rita illustrates how personality is shaped by social class, education and expectations about the role of the sexes in society, the gender roles.
The differences between men and women are categorised as follows:

1. *sex differences,* which are biological differences;
2. *gender differences,* meaning the different roles which men and women are expected to fulfil in a society.

In many societies, especially pre-industrial ones, it is regarded as natural for a woman to raise children and perform domestic tasks like cooking, collecting vegetables, carrying water and mending clothes. She is thought to be biologically equipped for such jobs and that her social role is simply the expression of her female nature. Men, on the other hand, with their superior physical strength, are seen as more suited to jobs such as hunting, mining, clearing land, chopping wood and building houses.
Sociologists are divided as to whether the sexual division of labour in society is really the result of biological differences or whether it is not due to cultural and social influences. Supporters of the latter view point out that children are prepared for their gender roles by parents, role models, the kind

of clothes they wear, their games, toys, and education in schools, colleges and at universities. Furthermore, they are constantly presented with stereotyped images of male and female roles by the mass media – in comics and magazines, on television and radio and in advertisements.

Traditional gender stereotypes and social roles

Some of the stereotypes traditionally associated with masculinity and femininity are:

– masculine: hard, logical, brave, aggressive, unemotional, independent
– feminine: soft, illogical, timid, passive, emotional, dependent.

This categorisation forms the basis of the social roles which each sex is supposed to fulfil. Men have been expected to take on important "public" positions such as businessmen, lawyers, doctors, government ministers and army generals – the type of work which calls for expertise, initiative and cool-headedness. Other "male" jobs are those demanding physical strength and courage, like builders, miners and firefighters. Women, on the other hand, have traditionally been allotted a more "private" role in which they were not expected to lead or create, but to serve others, particularly as housewives and mothers, but also as nurses, typists and junior school teachers.

The road towards equality between the sexes

In British history there are very few examples of women with influential roles in society – hardly any political leaders, famous writers, artists or scientists. Even as late as the beginning of the twentieth century they suffered from serious discrimination in every important area, legal, political, economic and social.

Modern women take freedom and equal rights for granted, but it has taken many years and long, hard struggles for women to progress so far. Some of the landmarks along this road are shown in the following chart.

1857–82	For the first time married women were allowed to own various kinds of possessions.
1874	Girton College for Women was set up at Cambridge, but women were not allowed full degrees until 1948.
1880	The Trade Union Congress adopted the principle of equal pay for women.
1882	Married women were given legal control over any income which they earned themselves.
1887	A nationwide group (The National Union of Women's Suffrage Society) campaigned for women's right to vote.
1918	Women over 30 were allowed to vote in general elections; the first women joined the police.
1928	Women over 21 could vote. They now had the same voting rights as men.
1958	The first women peers were allowed in the House of Lords.
1969	The new Open University gave access to higher education to adults who had formerly been excluded from it.
1970	Women were given the right to the same pay as men if they were doing similar work for the same employer (Equal Pay Act).
1972	Women were allowed to run in races longer than 400m in the Olympic Games.
1975	The Sex Discrimination Act enforced the 1970 Equal Pay Act.
1979	Margaret Thatcher became the first woman Prime Minister. She was one of only 19 female MPs out of 635.
1987	The first woman judge was appointed to the Court of Appeal.
1992	The first woman became Speaker of the House of Commons.
1994	The first women priests in the Church of England.
1997	The first Minister for Women, Harriet Harman.
2005	General Election results: 127 women MPs (out of 646) were voted into the House of Commons.
2006	Women still earn 17% less than men doing the same job.

In recent years further important steps have been taken against sexual discrimination:

- Many publishers and librarians gave priority to children's stories with girls in active, adventurous roles.
- Many advertisements now feature "liberated" women, such as career women drinking Guinness.
- Many schools actively campaign against sexism.
- Companies and educational institutions have introduced positive discrimination programmes to promote greater opportunities for women.

Yet women still have a long way to go on the road to complete equality. Although the Equal Pay Act (1970) and the Sexual Discrimination Act (1975) made men and women equal before the law, in reality the legislation is weak. At work, women are still on average paid less than men, they are less likely to be promoted and more likely to have part-time and/or low paid work. Women are also still expected to carry out most domestic tasks.

A 1994 trade union advertisement for women's rights

Girls are outperforming boys in education up to A-level. Although the number of female undergraduates has risen dramatically over the last 30 years women remain reluctant to pursue careers in science and engineering and they are still badly underrepresented in top positions such as the higher ranks of the civil service, local government, business executives, university chancellors and Members of Parliament.

The changing role of men

The emancipation of women has also forced men to change. Although many found this extremely distasteful they had no choice but to hand over a certain amount of legal, political and economic power to women.

One all-important milestone on the road to women's emancipation was the invention of the contraceptive pill, which was widely available by the end of the 1960s. Besides giving women control over pregnancies it also changed

them psychologically, allowing them to develop a more liberated, self-confident attitude to sexual pleasure.
As women had fewer children they stayed at work longer, which had huge consequences for the role of the man in the home. It took a long time for men – and society – to get used to the idea of men pushing prams and doing household chores. Gradually, however, the male stereotype changed and now it is more acceptable for men to show the softer side of their nature. Some have found this liberating, but others cannot cope with the breakdown of traditional gender roles. Deprived of their old role models they have to learn to define themselves in a new way.

Gender Roles in *Educating Rita*

Rita

Rita is an example of a young woman caught between the traditional stereotype of a woman's role and the then relatively new concept of an "emancipated" woman. Since the pill already existed Rita had more freedom of choice than her mother's generation. However, she is prevented from taking full control of her own life by the expectations of her working class environment.
The kind of people Rita lives among have not had the sort of education which has taught them to question basic assumptions. To them it is "natural" that young women like Rita should accept her role of wife and mother. They cannot even understand her doubts. Indeed, since Rita has no other role model it is rather surprising that she should be able to recognise the limiting nature of her lifestyle. Yet she feels frustrated and out of place and believes that the key to a more meaningful life lies in education.
The question arises why Rita did not make more of her educational opportunities while at school. The answer to this again lies in the stereotyped ideas about the role of girls and women in society. The people around her, adults and children, did not question conventional ideas about a woman's role and so discouraged girls from taking too much interest in education. Rita tells Frank about the pressures to conform:

> RITA. […] See, if I'd started takin' school seriously I would have had to become different from me mates, an that's not allowed.
> FRANK. By whom?
> RITA. By your mates, by your family, by everyone […]. (p. 31, ll. 6–10)

Denny

Rita's husband, Denny, cannot understand his wife's unwillingness to live the same kind of life as all the other young women in the neighbourhood. Unlike Rita, he has never thought about existential questions such as the quality of life. His behaviour towards Rita illustrates the enormous amount of pressure which can be exerted on those who do not conform to traditional ways of life.

Rita's refusal to accept conventional norms completely confuses Denny. His inflexibility of thought leaves him no alternative but to reject these unfamiliar ideas. He deals with the conflict in the only way he has learned and according to the typically "male" way of handling problems with wives and girlfriends – he grows angry and issues an ultimatum.

Denny is an example of many men who had difficulty in adapting to women's increasing demands for equality. When conventional patterns of thought and behaviour began to break down they were confused and afraid. Men in this position have two choices – either they succeed in adapting to the new ideas and redefine their relationships with women, or they stick to the old ideas. Faced with Denny's opposition anyone less determined than Rita would have given in. However, her education has liberated her so much that she cannot go back to a situation in which others are in control of her life. Because of Rita's determination and Denny's inflexibility their marriage is doomed to failure.

Trish

During Rita's search for more personal freedom she gets to know Trish and eventually moves in with her. Trish provides Rita with a completely different role model to the ones she is familiar with, such as her mother and the other women from her working class background. Trish is an extreme example of the new independent, "emancipated" type of woman. She helps to broaden Rita's outlook on life by introducing her to new people and new interests. With Trish's help Rita begins to feel at home with the better educated middle classes. However, her flatmate's attempted suicide brings Rita down to earth, making her realise that it is no good copying other people, but that she alone can define what kind of a person she wants to be and the type of life she wants to lead.

Frank

Frank illustrates the "new" type of man who has managed to adjust to the changing demands of women. He is the very opposite of the traditional "masculine" man. Although he is in a typically "male" profession as regards public power and influence, he is not at all interested in social prestige. His love of poetry and his insistence that emotions should not be suppressed when reacting to literature also negate the traditional stereotype about the "hard, unemotional" male psyche.

Frank's relationship with Rita illustrates how some men have changed as a result of women's demands for equality. Unlike Denny, Frank does not try to force his own views on Rita. Although he is not convinced she is doing the right thing he allows her the freedom to make her own decisions.

Setting

The whole play is set in Frank's office at the university where he teaches literature. The university itself is "Victorian-built" and in the north of England. Whilst the geographical location reflects the author's preference for writing about people from his own part of the country, the type of building is associated with long-standing traditions. It underlines the theme of the traditional approach to literary studies at British universities. Frank's office is full of the books and papers which he needs for his work. Rita loves the room because it has "taste". It represents the "better culture" she is seeking. Although she finds it a mess, she feels that it is somehow genuine, "there's nothing phoney about it" (p. 28, l. 9). She tells Frank that this is the sort of room she wants to have one day. Her question, "How d' y' make a room like this?" (p. 28, l. 3) could be interpreted as "How do I become the cultured kind of person who would have this kind of room?"

University like the one Frank teaches at

Rita's reaction to Frank's room is very significant because as she begins to acquire her "better culture" she moves into a flat with a young woman who also has the "right" books on her shelves. But in contrast to Frank's room, that of her flatmate does not reflect a genuinely well-educated person, but one who has only acquired superficial knowledge and opinions. Whereas at the beginning of the play Rita instinctively recognises the true education and culture of Frank's environment, later she becomes blinded by pretentiousness and second-hand ideas. And indeed, Frank's shelves are well stocked with classical authors such as T. S. Eliot, Dickens and Chekhov. There is also a painting of a nude religious scene, which Rita immediately notices. The vocabulary she uses, also the fact that she mentions it at all, shows that she is a very direct, outspoken sort of person. The print is important, too, because of its "good" quality. Rita is probably aware of the difference between the type of nude pictures which educated, cultured people have on their walls and the ones which she normally sees around her. By referring to the picture so openly she may also be testing Frank, as she does by swearing in front of him.

Frank's room not only illustrates the kind of work he does, but also the type of person he is, an intellectual with a thirst for reading and knowledge, and careless about conventional norms such as tidiness. The only non-intellectual note are the bottles of whisky hidden behind the books. They are an expression of his need to escape from his sense of futility and his lack of conviction about his social role. The coffee mug from which he drinks his whisky is a concession to his superiors. They know about his habit and are prepared to tolerate it as long as he keeps up appearances. There is a parallel between the university authorities and Denny, who also prefers to pretend that everything is fine instead of facing up to problems (see Theme 5).

Another important feature of Frank's room is the window, which Rita says she loves. Through it she can see all the "proper" students reading and studying on the lawn below. This view represents her idealised projections about educated people. Her wishful thinking forms a sharp contrast to Frank's disillusionment, "I sometimes get an urge to throw something through it. [...] A student usually" (p. 16, ll. 6–9). Frank hardly ever notices the view, but takes it for granted, just as he no longer notices the picture on the wall. This must seem like a mockery to Rita, who envies him his room so much. Because she is still in awe of universities and lecturers she does not recognise Frank's remark as his desire to escape from a world which he finds confining. Ironically, the same room represents freedom to the one person and imprisonment to the other.

The window takes on an additional symbolic meaning later in the play. In the first scene Frank describes Rita as "the first breath of air that's been in this room for years" (p. 22, ll. 16–17). However, when she tries to open it in Act II, scene 1, it is stuck. It seems that with her refreshing originality gone, she is no longer able to let any air in. The window also has a symbolic meaning with regards to Frank. He is unhappy with the limitations imposed on him by traditional approaches to literature. A poet at heart, he inwardly rebels against teaching students the accepted ways of "appreciating" literary works. But since he cannot live by writing poetry he has no other option. His sense of imprisonment is expressed in his physical environment.

Frank's room signifies both imprisonment and his retreat from the world.

Not only is his window permanently closed, but it is also difficult to open the door from the outside. So other people cannot enter easily. Just as Rita feels imprisoned by her home environment, Frank is confined to a job he dislikes, symbolised by his confinement to one single room. The fact that Rita has difficulties opening Frank's door could also be read as a symbolic barrier preventing her from entering his world. Frank's only other social contacts, apart from Rita, are his students and Julia, his partner, but none of these relationships seem very satisfactory. Rita, on the other hand, is connected with several different locations, although we only hear about them – her home, the pub, the hairdressing salon and bistro where she works and summer school. Consequently, her social contacts are many and varied. Whereas Frank is only associated with one setting throughout the play, Rita's physical location changes as she moves from the home she shares with her husband to her mother's and then to a flat.

It is interesting that neither Frank nor Rita are able to enter the other's private sphere. Frank invites Rita to his home, but she feels unable to enter. Similarly, he would not be at home in her environment. This total separation between the physical locations could be interpreted as a symbol of the gulf which exists between the social classes. Both are completely ignorant of each other's home environment and interaction on a private level is impossible. It is only with great difficulty that Rita finally manages to penetrate into Frank's world.

Besides the window and door, another feature of Frank's room which takes on symbolic significance is his chair. During their first tutorials Frank always sits in a swivel chair. On one occasion he offers it to Rita, but she declines, saying, "No. You're the teacher, you sit there" (p. 27, l. 26). It is interesting that Frank says it does not matter where he sits. He obviously does not need furniture to reinforce his authority. Later, however, after he turned up drunk to a lecture, he sits Rita down in his own chair and she no longer protests (p. 95, ll. 1–2). This underlines her feeling that she is now on the same level as him and, in the present situation, even superior.

Significantly, when Rita and Frank reach the end of their time together, the room is emptied. It is as if the stage is being cleared for a new beginning. The packing up of the books marks the end of the teacher-student relationship. Everything is being removed so that something else can take its place. The clearing of the room signifies the end of something, but also a new beginning. Like the room, both Rita's and Frank's lives will be filled with new contents, as yet unknown. In Frank's case, the ambiguity of his future is reinforced by his destination. Australia is a country where prisoners used to be sent, but it is also a relatively new country. As Frank himself says, "Things are just beginning there" (p. 110, ll. 4–5). Rita's future location is even more uncertain. She does not know where the next scene in her life will be set and, like Frank's room, does not know which people will be in it.

Symbolism

Russell makes frequent use of symbolism to give additional meaning to a point he is making. The most obvious example is Rita's changes of name to underline her transformation from Susan, the uneducated hairdresser, to Rita, the admirer of an author of popular fiction, and then back again to Susan, as she rejects her own pretentiousness and accepts herself as she is. It is significant that the author whom Russell selects as the object of Rita's admiration, Rita Mae Brown, was one of the founders of both the women's and the gay movement. Rita's admiration for her prepares the audience to expect similar traits in Rita's personality.

All the works which Russell chooses for Rita's education have a symbolic significance. The one she starts with, E. M. Forster's *Howards End*, is a parallel story to Rita's own: a young, working class man is living in poverty, but trying to educate himself. He knows that there is more to life than everyday existence and is searching for some deeper meaning to it. He loves literature and music, but the woman he lives with cannot understand him. By chance, he gets to know a wealthy, cultured family and at first tries to copy them. Eventually, however, he progresses beyond mere imitation. One element which is particularly relevant to Rita's story is a woman who acts as a link between different social classes. When her leisurely, cultured life is disrupted, she at first feels disoriented and isolated, but then manages to reconcile two apparently conflicting ways of life.

Russell's choice of *Howards End* is also significant because of the now famous phrase with which Forster introduced it "only connect". As Rita's mind becomes better trained she is increasingly able to make new connections between various different phenomena. Frank proves to her, for instance, that her description of working class life is actually an illustration of the phrase (pp. 50–51).

When Rita suggests that the phrase describes how "no-one does connect" in the novel (p. 51, l. 29) she is also unconsciously describing her own situation and that of Frank. At home Rita cannot connect in any meaningful way with those around her and the same can be said of Frank. As the play develops, the relationship between Rita and Frank deteriorates and they, too, find that they can no longer connect with each other. The phrase is also a comment on Rita as she is at the end of the play, when she seems able to combine her past with her present. After a period of alienation from her original background, she can contemplate spending Christmas at her parents'.

Having finally come to terms with *Howards End*, Rita moves on to Ibsen's play *Peer Gynt*. Again, this choice underlines Rita's own situation. She herself refers to it as the story of someone "searchin' for the meaning of life" (p. 48, ll. 28–29). At the end of the nineteenth century Ibsen shocked audiences with his realism and by writing about topics such as a woman's right to leave her husband and create her own life.

After Ibsen, she progresses to Chekhov, a dramatist whose characters cannot relate to each other and who hide the frustation and emptiness of their lives behind a facade. This choice of author is an indirect comment on the lives of most of the characters in *Educating Rita* – Rita herself, Frank, Mrs White and Trish. Rita's increasing familiarity with Chekhov underlines the breakup of her relationship with Frank.

During the summer school course Rita not only learns about Chekhov, but also about the poet William Blake. Once more, Russell is making an indirect comment on her progress. Blake wrote two sets of poems, the *Songs of Innocence* and the *Songs of Experience*. The first set, the *Songs of Innocence*, describes ideals and childlike innocence; the second is often bitter in tone and shows how these ideals turn into illusions in the face of reality. Tellingly, the poem which Rita learns off by heart, "The Sick Rose", is one of the *Songs of Experience*. This choice of poems gives additional significance to Rita's progression from a state of innocence regarding the study of literature to one of experience. But the selection of a poem from the second collection could be a hint that her dreams might not be fulfilled, or at least not in the way she expects.

Another interesting literary reference is to a novel by W. Somerset Maugham, *Of Human Bondage* (1915). Although only briefly mentioned, it touches on one of the main ideas of the play, that of imprisonment. Both Rita and Frank feel imprisoned by their environment and, eventually, both manage to escape. In Frank's case Russell's choice of Australia as his new destination might be a hint that he is really only exchanging one "prison" for another. There are many feature of Frank's office which symbolically reinforce this theme (see Setting).

Besides Rita's changes of name, the most overt symbol of her progress is in the last scene, when Frank "rewards" her with a present of a dress "for an educated woman friend" (p. 111, l. 7). This is a reminder that when Rita started her course she vowed not to buy a new dress until she had passed her first exam and then it would be "a proper dress, the sort of dress you'd only see on an educated woman" (p. 32, ll. 16–17). Frank's present acknowledges her successful transformation into just such a person.

Structure

The play consists of a series of conversations between Rita and her tutor, Frank, all set in Frank's university office. It traces the process by which the two get to know each other and at the same time discover themselves. Because attention is focussed on psychological processes rather than events the pace is rather slow. Given the limited number of characters and settings it is interesting how Russell still manages to sustain the audience's interest. The first meeting between the two characters is very lively and amusing, partly because of Rita's outspokenness and sense of humour, and partly because of some comical misunderstandings arising from discrepancies in their knowledge of literature.

As the first Act progresses the tone becomes more serious. Rita realises how much she has to learn and Frank becomes increasingly aware of the huge responsibility he has taken on. Variety is provided by the introduction of Rita's husband, Denny. Although he never actually appears, his presence is felt very strongly because of the restrictions he imposes on his wife's studies. Denny is an underlying source of tension, keeping the audience wondering if Rita will manage to continue with her education in the face of his growing opposition. The conflict between husband and wife gradually escalates up to the point where Denny burns Rita's books (scene 5). However, the mood quickly reverts to one of calm when Rita insists on discussing her work instead of her marriage.

Throughout the play Frank and Rita's conversations about literature are interspersed with information about their private lives. This provides a variety of different topics, thus sustaining the audience's interest. One example of this alternation between academic subjects and personal details is Act I, scene 6, which begins rather startlingly when Rita bursts unexpectedly into Frank's office. The explanation is that she was so overwhelmed by a production of *Macbeth* the night before that she had to come and tell him about it. Typically, the conversation switches from the personal to the academic as Frank takes the opportunity to explain the dramatic meaning of the term "tragic".

Towards the end of the first Act Rita's education takes a more serious turn when she suddenly realises that she is now in a no-man's-land, belonging neither to her original culture, nor to Frank's academic world. Rita, like the play itself, has arrived at a half-way mark and we wonder yet again whether she will be able to fulfil her dream of finding a "better culture". The crisis deepens because of Frank's lack of understanding. A calmer mood is introduced with Rita's decision, at the end of scene 7, to carry on with her education. But just as the audience settles back, imagining that things will run a little more smoothly from now on, another crisis arises. This time it is Denny who has provoked it by throwing his wife out. As before, Rita refuses to discuss the problem and the conversation reverts to her studies.

By the end of the first Act the play and Rita have reached a half-way stage. For her there is no alternative but to go on with her studies. She has become alienated from her original, working class environment and her marriage is over. The end of the first Act also represents a half-way point for Frank, because this is his last chance to decide whether to accept the responsibility of teaching Rita, with all that it entails, or not. His periodic doubts about teaching her during Act I give the play an additional source of tension.

Educating Rita is a very symmetrical work. It is divided roughly into two halves, the first dealing more with Rita and the second with Frank. This symmetry is underlined by parallels in the development of both characters. Both feel alienated from and imprisoned by their original environments and in both cases their relationships with their partners break down. Rita's two crises towards the end of Act I are paralleled in Act II by Frank's increasing despair, which culminates in an enforced sabbatical.

After Rita's crises in Act I the second half of the play starts off in a more settled way. A course at summer school has firmly established Rita's identity as a student and Frank has apparently decided to continue teaching her. Interest now shifts to Frank. From the beginning of Act II he displays increasing signs of dissatisfaction with the "new" Rita. Tension between them mounts and eventually explodes in a clash over Rita's interpretation of a poem by William Blake in scene 3.

During the second Act the two characters grow further apart as they develop in opposite directions. The introduction of Rita's flatmate, Trish, revives interest and introduces a new theme. For Rita is so impressed by Trish's cultured lifestyle that she adopts her as a model. Later, Trish's suicide attempt is the catalyst which eventually leads to the restoration of good feelings between Rita and Frank.

As Rita gradually establishes her position in the academic world, Frank becomes increasingly unacceptable there. The disappearance of the "old" Rita makes him all the more conscious of the limitations and dangers of his university work. His deepening sense of despair and frustration and his growing need for alcohol finally lead to his professional downfall. Like Rita at the end of Act I, Frank is now in a state of crisis.

During this time Frank and Rita seem to exchange roles. Whereas Frank was the dominant partner in Act I, in the second Act it is Rita who gradually assumes this role. By the end of the play she feels thoroughly at home in Frank's world, whereas he has been expelled from it. Again there is a parallel to Rita's life, for at the end of Act I she, too, had been expelled from her original environment.

The tension between the two comes to a head in II,5 when Frank describes Rita as a monster. For a while there is almost no contact between them. In the following scene Russell uses the device of a telephone call to keep the action going, although there is only one person on stage.
The play ends on a harmonious, though ambiguous note. Rita and Frank have re-established their former relationship, but will go their separate ways, at least in the near future. This last scene emphasises the similarities between them. Both are at a crossroads. For both one phase of their lives is over and they must start on something new. Act I showed how they accompanied each other for a while, Act II described how they started to go different ways and now, at the end of the play, they have come together again. Besides the changing relationship between the two characters, the various stages of their separate developments provide a constant source of interest.

Style

The most striking features of Russell's style are his use of a strong Liverpool dialect and his sense of humour. Indeed one critic even speaks of his "sparkling Liverpool humour that has since become his trademark" (Charles, 1983, p. 21). Apart from a brief phase when Rita tries to imitate her flatmate's upper class way of speaking, she retains her Liverpool accent throughout the play. She does, however, drop the more vulgar expressions as she joins the ranks of the educated middle classes.

Language and Social Class

During the course of the play Rita's speech is affected by her studies. Having to analyse literature forces her to describe her reactions to it in a more differentiated way. At the beginning of her studies she finds it very difficult to put her thoughts into words and often has to fall back on "fillers" such as "y' know" and "like". Later, however, as her thinking becomes more differentiated, she expresses herself more precisely and more fluently.

Rita's early use of language is typical of the non-standard English used by the working class, especially the lower working class. Characteristic features of this variety of language are: a limited range of vocabulary, simple sentence structures, sentences often unfinished and the repeated use of "fillers" (y' know).

Rita's speech forms a sharp contrast with Frank's more formal standard English. He is able to put his thoughts together fluently in longer, more complicated sentences and does not need so many "fillers". His vocabulary is wider and more sophisticated and in comparison to Rita's sloppy pronunciation, his is more precise.

Rita is very conscious of the social prestige attached to the way educated people like Frank speak English. Since the beginning of the twentieth century the standardised accent which Frank uses, generally known as RP (Received Pronunciation), has been associated with a high social standing and a good education. Although RP is only spoken by about 3% of the population, its influence is enormous. Many people who have been brought up with regional dialects prefer to modify them in order to improve their chances of moving up in society or to make themselves more acceptable to their environment. Although the situation is less extreme than it used to be, dialect speakers can still find themselves at a disadvantage. Apparently, the most unacceptable accents are those of Liverpool ("Scouse"), Birmingham ("Brummie") and Glasgow:

> "The long-held suspicions of Scousers, Brummies and others that they suffer discrimination at work or when applying for jobs because of their accents has been borne out by new research. The accents of Liverpool, Glasgow and Birmingham are regarded by some employers as particularly 'negative', a survey of recruitment consultants has found [...] Former Arsenal and England footballer Alan Smith now writes on soccer for *The Daily Telegraph*, but fears his Birmingham accent would obstruct a move into broadcasting [...] Edwina Currie, Tory MP for Derbyshire South and originally from Liverpool, admitted to adapting her accent to the nature of her audience. She said, 'I used to have a really strong Scouse accent [...], but it has softened a bit now.'" (*The Weekly Telegraph*, 8.–14. Jan. 1997, p. 6)

As Rita begins to feel more at home in the academic world she modifies her language, dropping swear words and slang. Her speech begins to resemble the standard English which is characteristic of her new environment. Frank, on the other hand, is starting to sound more like Rita when she first appeared in his office. He swears, "Sod them – no, fuck them" (p. 92, l. 18), uses Rita's slangy expression "off my cake" (p. 94, l. 2) and even passes on Rita's initial definition of assonance, "gettin' the rhyme wrong" to his students (p. 17, l. 12; p. 94, ll. 16–17). It is as if he is symbolically rejecting the more sophisticated, academic mode of speech in favour of what he feels is the direct, less pretentious way in which people from Rita's background express themselves.

Humour

Much of the humour of the play derives from the clash of cultures expressed by the exchanges between Rita and Frank. The first scene provides many examples of the comical misunderstandings arising from their different levels of knowledge and education. Rita's entrance, for instance, is not typical of the quiet, respectful way in which a student would normally enter a tutor's room for the first time. Unexpectedly, the usual roles are reversed as the student takes the initiative and even accuses the teacher of negligence ("you wanna get it fixed", p. 8, l. 1).
The situational comedy of Rita's entrance results from the discrepancy between our expectations of a student's behaviour in these circumstances and Rita's inexperience of such situations. Their first exchange is comical because, again, Rita is not familiar with this kind of formal situation. She does not understand that Frank's enquiry "You are?" (p. 8, l. 12) is a request for her name and interprets it as a question about her personality. Rita does not know, either, that she should not really walk around inspecting the room or ask her tutor personal questions.
The discrepancy between Rita's and Frank's experience of life is reflected

not only in Rita's inappropriate behaviour, but also in her way of speaking. Her vocabulary is out of place in such a formal, academic situation. Besides swearing, for instance, she uses the vulgar expression "tits" (p. 9, l. 5) when describing a painting.

The humorous misunderstandings continue throughout the first scene as Rita fails to recognise Frank's literary references. To her Yeats is a wine bar, not the poet whose name is pronounced in the same way, and Eliot is a Chicago policeman, not T. S. Eliot, the poet. The comedy also results from Rita's own wit, such as her description of a middle class intellectual like Frank as "a Flora man" (p. 21, l. 14) or humorous remarks like "It'll probably have a job findin' my brain" (p. 12, l. 19).

Although Frank is rather shocked at Rita's behaviour he is also delighted, finding her natural spontaneity and originality refreshing. When he recovers from his initial bewilderment he realises that she is deliberately using bad language to test his tolerance, "If I'd got some other tutor I wouldn't have stayed. [...] someone who objected to swearin'" (p. 15, ll. 9–13). Frank's own dry, cynical sense of humour enables him to cope with Rita and provides another source of humour, such as in the following exchange (p. 41, ll. 9–14):

> RITA. This Forster, honest to God he doesn't half get on my tits.
> FRANK. Good. You must show me the evidence.

Bibliography

Text Editions

Russell, Willy: *Educating Rita.* London: Samuel French, 1981.

- *Educating Rita, Stags and Hens, and Blood Brothers. Two Plays and a Musical.* London: Methuen, 1988.
- *Educating Rita.* Harlow: Longman, 1991.
- *Educating Rita.* Frankfurt/Main: Diesterweg, 1997.
- *Educating Rita.* Stuttgart: Reclam, 1997.

Selected Bibliography

Allan, P. / Benyon, J. / McCormick, B. (eds.): *Focus on Britain 1994.* Oxford: Perennial Publications, 1994.

Chambers, C. / Prior, M.: *Playwrights' Progress.* Oxford: Amber Lane Press, 1987. [An analysis of post-war British drama. Russell is one of a group of playwrights whose aim is to broaden the class basis of the theatre. They concentrate on regional rather than mainstream theatre and write about class for working class audiences.]

Charles, Timothy: "The First Ten Years". In: *Drama* 2nd Quarter 1083, No. 148, pp. 20–21. Published by The British Theatre Association, London.

Debusscher, Gilbert: "*Educating Rita or an Open University Pygmalion*". In: G. D. / Jean Pierre van Noppen (eds.): *Communiquer et traduire: Hommages à Jean Dierickx / Communicating and translating: Essays in Honour of Jean Dierickx.* Bruxelles: Édition de L'Université de Bruxelles, 1985, pp. 303–317.

Dictionary of English Language and Culture. Harlow: Longman, 1992.

Gill, John: *Willy Russell and His Plays.* Birkenhead: Countyvise, 1996. [An extensive interview with Russell covering his dramas, his social background and his political intentions. Also includes descriptions of all his plays and a comprehensive bibliography.]

Glaap, A.-R.: *Willy Russell: "Educating Rita". Comments and Study Aids.* Frankfurt/Main: Diesterweg, 1984. [A short collection of comments and study aids on *Educating Rita* and a lengthy interview with Russell himself.]

Jones, Christopher N.: *Populism, the Mainstream Theatre, and the Plays of Willy Russell.* UMI Dissertation Information Services. Ann Arbor (Mich.) 1989. [An analysis of the relationship between popular theatre and contemporary mainstream British theatre, with Russell as a representative of the former. Includes an extensive interview with Russell.]

The Spectator: "We are doing very well, thank you", 13 March 1993, p. 10.

The Times Higher Educational Supplement: "What Rita lost along with the shampoo and sets", 4 July 1980.

Townroe, C. / Yates, G.: *Sociology.* Harlow: Longman, 1995.

The Weekly Telegraph: "How you say things puts the accent on success", 8.–14. January 1997, p. 6.

Ziegésar, Detlef and Margaret von: *Grundwissen. Landeskunde United Kingdom.* Stuttgart: Ernst Klett Verlag, 2000. Chapter 8: "Social Structure", pp. 84–98.

Model Tasks with Answers

The following tasks illustrate the influence of society, family, peer groups and institutions on the behaviour of men and women and show how these factors shape gender roles much more than biological differences between the sexes. The tasks are divided into four main sections:

- the influence of social background: family, friends and neighbours,
- the influence of school,
- breaking out of a restrictive environment,
- Rita's choices.

The tasks are based on the workbook Detlef and Margaret von Ziegésar, *Willy Russell, "Educating Rita". Arbeitsblätter Englisch,* Stuttgart: Klett, 1997. Further tasks on other aspects of the play are also contained in this workbook.

I The Influence of Social Background: Family, Friends and Neighbours

1. Rita tells Frank that she feels "out of step" with the people around her (p. 23, l. 5). The term "out of step" is taken from dancing and suggests that someone is dancing to a different tune or rhythm to everyone else.
Explain what Rita means with regard to
a) her family, her friends and the neighbours
b) her husband.

a) At 26, Rita is frustrated with her life. She is a hairdresser and has not had much of an education. Her social circle, family, friends and neighbours, expect no more of her than that she should have children and provide a good home for her family. Rita, however, finds this kind of life limiting and wants more. She does not know exactly what she wants, but is looking for more meaning in life, more choices.
Rita cannot talk to the people around her because they do not understand her needs. She tells Frank that although she talks a lot to him, at home she does not say much. She finds it easier to talk to Frank because she feels he understands her and is interested in the same things as she is (p. 16, ll. 15–18).

b) Among the people Rita feels "out of step" with is her husband, Denny. He expects her to behave like all the other young women in the neighbourhood and have a baby. Rita, however, does not want a baby, at least not yet. First she wants to discover herself, realise her own potential and find out what other choices she has in life besides staying at home with a baby. Denny cannot understand these needs.

2. Explain how Rita feels about her customers and describe the dramatic function of the customers.

Rita finds her customers arrogant, describing them as "stuck-up idiots" (p. 14, l. 19). Although she sometimes hates them (p. 15, l. 5), she does not blame them, "It's not their fault; they can't help it", p. 15, l. 4. She realises that they lead narrow, limited lives because they have had no opportunity to see that there are alternatives.
The customers are not important in their own right, but in the dramatic function they fulfil in the play. They are a "dramatic foil" to Rita, meaning that by contrasting them with Rita Russell is able to put more emphasis on his heroine's actions.

Rita criticises her customers for believing that they can change themselves by simply altering their hairstyles, "they come to the hairdresser's cos they wanna be changed" (p. 22, l. 1). The women's superficial attitude to change throws into sharp relief Rita's deeper search for a new kind of life, one which will involve her whole personality, "if you want to change y' have to do it from the inside, don't y'? […] like I'm doin'" (p. 22, ll. 2–3). She has begun this process of change by enrolling for the university course.

3. **Russell uses an extended metaphor to explain what the course means to Rita. Give examples of images expressing this metaphor. Find a metaphor to show how Rita imagines her life without the university course.**

Give …
Rita feels that in order to provide herself with more choices in life she needs a better education and so signs on for a literature course at the Open University. The course opens up a whole new world to her by giving her insights into a different culture. In fact, the course becomes so important to her that it begins to represent life itself. This is expressed by a series of metaphors linked to the idea of the course giving her life: "it's providin' me with life itself. […] it's given me more life than I've had in years" (p. 55, ll. 18–21); "you give me room to breathe. Y' […] feed me" (p. 54, ll. 15–16).

Find …
Rita says that her husband "wants to take life away from me; he wants me to stop rockin' the coffin" (p. 55, ll. 18–20). This expresses her belief that if she did not have the course she would feel she did not have any life at all. The phrase "rockin' the coffin" is a reference to the saying "rocking the boat", which means causing a disturbance and thus endangering a boat at sea. Rita is implying that Denny sees her rebellion against tradition as a danger to the stability of their life. By using the word "coffin" instead of "boat" Rita is implying that her old way of life resembles death (p. 55, ll. 20–24).

4. Explain why Frank's invitation to Denny and Rita provokes a crisis. Consider both Denny's and Rita's reactions. Was Frank right to invite Rita to dinner or was he naive and thoughtless?

Explain ...
By inviting Denny and Rita to dinner at his house Frank provokes a crisis. Rita tells Frank, "We had a big fight about it" (p. 69, l. 3).

Denny
Denny probably feels that he is being forced to choose between his familiar lifestyle and that of Frank. Like Rita, he would feel extremely uncomfortable in the company of people like Frank and Julia, whose lifestyles are so completely different from his own. However, unlike his wife, Denny is not even willing to try to enlarge his experience of life.

Rita
The invitation not only provokes a crisis in the relationship between Rita and her husband, but also within Rita herself. The difficulties already start when she is getting ready to go out. Because she has never been to a middle class dinner party before she has no idea what clothes to wear or what kind of wine to take. She is also worried that she will not be able to make the appropriate kind of conversation and that the others will laugh at her.
These psychological difficulties are underlined by the physical ones of not being able to find her way to the house. Finally, standing outside looking in, Rita realises that she does not fit in with Frank's social environment, "I saw y' all through the window, y' were sippin' drinks an' talkin' an' laughin'. An' I couldn't come in" (p. 69, ll. 18–20). But Rita also realises that she is now even more alienated from people than before, belonging to neither her original social group nor the one she was aspiring to, "I'm a freak. I can't talk to the people I live with any more. An' I can't talk to the likes of them on Saturday, or them out there, because I can't learn the language. I'm a half-caste" (p. 71, ll. 19–22).
When Rita says she "can't learn the language" of people like Frank she is not only referring to a certain way of speaking, but also to the attitudes, values and lifestyle which generally characterise academic circles. Having decided that she will never be able to change enough to fit in with them, she decides to give up her studies and, with it, her attempt to create a more meaningful life for herself. In an attempt to at least try to connect once more with her own kind of people she turns away from the dinner party and goes to join her family and friends in the pub.

Was Frank right …?
Judging by Frank's dislike of academics he probably was not looking forward to the evening very much and thought he would enjoy it more if Rita came. Out of politeness he had to invite Denny, too, although he probably did not expect to have much in common with him. However, Frank could be accused of selfishness and insensitivity for not foreseeing the embarrassment he would cause Rita. He should have known, too, that it would cause conflict between her and her husband.

5. Put these characters in groups to show which belong together and which are outsiders: Rita, Frank, Denny, the people in the pub, Rita's mother, Julia, the dinner guests. Give reasons for your decisions.

Denny and the people in the pub form a group, not only because they all share the same working class background, but also because they have the same attitudes to life.
Rita's mother, although she undoubtedly belongs to the people in the pub, is slightly outside her group. Like Rita she also senses that life has passed her by and that she has missed out on something. We do not know exactly how she feels about Rita's studies but her behaviour in the pub implies that she understands her daughter's feelings. Rita interprets her mother's regretful "we could sing better songs than those" (p. 72, ll. 18–19) as a wish that she herself had been able to choose a different lifestyle.
Julia and the dinner guests can be grouped together because they have the same middle class background, together with the values and lifestyle which go with it.
Rita belongs to neither group. She feels alienated from both her original working class background and from academics like Frank and Julia.
Frank, too, is an outsider. Although he loves literature he is disillusioned by academic life. Most of his students do not share his love of his subject, "appalling teaching is quite in order for most of my appalling students" (p. 25, ll. 6–7). Frank also dislikes conventional teaching methods because they often take the joy out of learning. Rita is surprised at his lack of enthusiasm for education, "Y'd think there was somethin' wrong with education to hear you talk" – "Perhaps there is" (p. 39, ll. 11–13). Frank so rarely meets people like Rita, with her genuine love of learning and original ideas, that he finds her tremendously refreshing, "you're the first breath of air that's been in this room for years" (p. 22, ll. 16–17).

6. **When Rita joined her family in the pub she had made up her mind not to continue with her studies (p. 71, ll. 24–25). Explain why she changed her mind and decided to continue with them. Discuss the sacrifices she will probably have to make.**
   How do Rita's and Denny's reactions to the mother's tears reveal their characters?

When Rita ...
Rita interprets her mother's tears in the pub as frustration and unhappiness with her way of life. This strengthens Rita's determination not to lead as narrow a life as her mother. She knows that this will be painful because it will alienate her even more from her original environment. Because those around her will not understand her decision she will not receive any help or sympathy from them. However, it is more important to her to take control of her own life and to have more choice in what she does.

How ...?
Denny may understand his mother-in-law's frustration and disappoinment, but prefers to ignore it, pretending nothing has happened. He does not want to think about problems, but prefers a facade of happiness to the truth. Unlike his wife, he does not have the courage to change things.

7. **Describe the dramatic function of Rita's mother. Give the main reason why young women like Rita already had more freedom of choice in their lives than their mothers and discuss the implication of this choice in your own society today.**

Rita's mother is not so important in her own right as in contrast to Rita (she is a "dramatic foil" to Rita). In her disappointment and frustration at the emptiness of her life she serves as a mirror to her daughter, warning her what sort of life she can expect if she follows convention. It is too late for the mother to change anything, but not for Rita.
Young women of Rita's generation were able to choose whether to have children or not. When their mothers were of child-bearing age the pill had not yet been invented.
The impact of the pill made a huge difference to the choices women had in life and revolutionised the roles of men and women in society. Today many young women enjoy a good education and prefer to spend some years working before having children. They tend to have fewer children than their mothers and have them later. Many decide not to have children at all. Despite the changing perceptions of men and women's roles it is still mostly the women who are responsible for bringing up children and it is

not always easy to combine having children with going out to work. One enormous difficulty is that there are not enough provisions for child care and that schools and kindergardens are only open a few hours a day.

8. **Look at the cover of this 1955 magazine and describe in note form how female and male roles are presented.**

Imagine you have to create an advertisement for a washing machine. What would it be like? Think about:

- **the setting;**
- **the kind of people in the advertisement: women, men, children, their ages;**

- **what the people look like, their styling of dressing;**
- **what the people are doing; the kind of activities they are associated with;**
- **where everyone is: which people are near to each other, how they relate to each other;**
- **the expressions on the people's faces;**
- **their gestures; the feelings they are expressing;**
- **a caption or other written message.**

The cover presents a picture of the ideal family as it was perceived in the 1950s – two parents with two children, the woman at home and the man going out to work. Today, by contrast, this idea of a nuclear family has broken down. There are many different models of family life – one-parent families, patchwork families, couples without children and single households.

FEMALE	MALE
• Woman as housewife and mother. Set in traditional women's domain, kitchen. Children round woman. Caption "Mum's dream" emphasises role. Also shows limitations of women's aims in life (choices).	• Men go to work, earn money. Men associated with technology.
• Wife financially dependent on husband, passive role, grateful for men's help and skills. Reinforced by second woman looking in through window.	• Husband as provider, giving wife one of the new labour-saving devices at the time, a washing machine.
• Girl with doll, preparation for domestic role.	• Boy has toy cart, preparation for type of job.
• Girl offers doll's clothes for washing – interested in practical household matters.	• Boy looking at machine – interested in technology.

II The Influence of School

**9. List some quotations from Act 1, scene 2 to show the kind of pressures Rita was under at school. Describe these pressures in your own words.
Find a longer passage in this scene in which Rita explains why people pressurised her in this way.**

List …
The following quotations illustrate the pressure to conform which was exerted on Rita by those around her:

- None of Rita's classmates were interested in school, or at least they did not say they were, "studyin' was just for the wimps, wasn't it? See, if I'd started takin' school seriously I would have had to become different from me mates, an' that's not allowed. […] So y' never admit that school could be anythin' other than useless" (p. 31, ll. 5–12).
- The pressure to reject school was not only exerted by Rita's classmates, but by her whole environment, "that's not allowed. […] By your mates, by your family, by everyone" (p. 31, ll. 8–10). If Rita had worked hard at school or even shown much interest in it she would have been rejected by everyone around her. She would have been an outsider.

Find …
The people Rita lives among want her to be like themselves. For her to show an interest in school work would be regarded as a rejection of their way of life. They would feel that their values were being questioned and even threatened. Rita herself explains that it was easier to pretend she had no problems than to try to solve them, "There's always somethin' to make you forget about it. So y' do, y' keep goin', tellin' yourself life's great. […] y' have to decide whether it's gonna be another change of dress or a change in yourself. An' it's really temptin' to go out an' get another dress […] it doesn't upset anyone around y'. Like cos they don't want y' to change" (p. 31, ll. 21–23; p. 32, ll. 5–10).

Additional information:

The importance of education for personal development is a thread running through Russell's work. Most of his plays are about people trying to escape from the culture they were born into. In fact, *Educating Rita* has strong biographical elements because Russell himself dropped out of school at 15. Like Rita, he became a hairdresser. Later he returned to school, took some exams at night school and then trained to be a drama teacher.
Russell is bitter about the fact that those at the bottom end of the social scale have been deprived of a good education and of the chance to participate more fully in cultural life. He feels that they have not been offered the opportunities to make meaningful choices about the kind of lives they would like to lead.

**10. Which reasons for Rita's failure at school are suggested by this song?
Explain why the girl finds the question "What would you like to be?" annoying ("they had the nerve").
Do you think things have changed much since the time when this song appeared?**

When I went to school I learned to write and how to read.
Some history, geography and home economy,
And typing is a skill that every girl is sure to need,
To while away the extra time until the time to breed,
And then they had the nerve to say, "What would you like to be?"
NO, YOU ONLY NEED TO LEARN TO BE A LADY.
THE DUTY ISN'T YOURS, FOR TO TRY AND RUN THE WORLD,
AN ENGINEER COULD NEVER HAVE A BABY,
REMEMBER, DEAR, THAT YOU'RE A GIRL.

(Adams/Laurikietietis, *The Gender Trap*, London: Quartet Books, 1976, p. 16)

l. 2 **home economy:** how to run a home (shopping, cooking etc.)
l. 4 **to while away the extra time:** to spend the spare time in a pleasant, lazy way
to breed: to have young (mostly used for animals)
l. 5 **to have the nerve:** to be annoying or rude
l. 7 **the duty isn't yours, for to ...:** it isn't your job to ...

Which reasons …?
Girls from Rita's background were generally not encouraged to get a good education. They were expected to marry, have children and stay at home. But the song also suggests a further reason for Rita's failure at school, namely the stereotyped expectations of the kind of knowledge and skills girls needed to learn – a little history and geography, but also home economics so that they could run a home. Typing, too, was regarded as a useful skill, although it could only lead to a relatively unskilled job. In any case girls were only expected to go out to work until they had children ("to while away …").

Explain …
The girl finds the question "What would you like to be?" annoying and ironic in view of the limited choices which girls are offered. She could not, for example, be an engineer because of the stereotype that it is not a job for a girl.

Do you think …?
- Some stereotyped ideas about gender still discourage both boys and girls from doing certain jobs.
- In the past women's access to education has been limited. For instance, it was not until 1874 that a college for women was set up at Cambridge University in England and they were not allowed to take full degrees until 1948.
- Feminists have argued that children are conditioned from birth for their adult roles as men and women. They have often criticised education for reinforcing gender roles by suggesting that certain jobs or professions are more suitable for one sex than the other. Traditionally, women have been trained for the more "caring" type of work such as nursing, teaching young children and social work.
- Interestingly, although girls usually do better at school than boys, in later life women are vastly outnumbered by men in the higher ranks of most professions.

III Breaking out of a Restrictive Environment

11. Suggest reasons why Rita chose the Open University to do her literature course.

Because students of the Open University (founded in 1969) can study from home it is suitable for people like Rita who have to go to work or for those with children. Teaching is by a mixture of printed materials, television and radio programmes. Each student is given a tutor, like Frank, whom they see regularly. He sets them tasks, they post him their work and he marks it and discusses it with them.
It is always difficult for adults to pursue higher education because of the conflicting demands of jobs and home life, but generally women have more problems than men. This is not only because of the difficulties of combining studies and home life, but also in view of the expectations of their social environment, especially if they come from Rita's kind of background.

**12. Look at Act 1, scenes 4 and 5 and describe Denny's reactions to his wife's studies. How does Rita feel about her husband?
Describe the way Denny and Frank relate to Rita from the point of view of gender roles.**

Look at …

- Denny does not like Rita studying at home (p. 46, ll. 18–19).
- He tried to stop her seeing Frank (p. 51, l. 14), wanting her to go out with him and his friends instead.
- Denny wants Rita to stop taking the pill and have a baby, like all the other young women in the neigbourhood. He resents her studies so much that he burns her books and homework (p. 53, ll. 16–17).
- He is jealous of what Frank can give his wife and may even suspect that they are having an affair (p. 54, ll. 20–21).
- Denny cannot understand that Rita wants more meaningful choices in life than materialistic ones (p. 55, ll. 24 ff.).
- Rita thinks Denny feels threatened and disoriented because she is doing something unusual. He is afraid because she is becoming a more independent person and challenging traditional ideas, "It makes me stronger comin' here. That's what Denny's frightened of" (p. 51, ll. 18–19). Denny wants his wife to behave like himself in order to reinforce his own values and justify his own way of life. He feels she is betraying him and her social origins by no longer accepting their kind of life ("He said I'd betrayed him", p. 73, l. 21). He is afraid of change.

- Rita understands Denny's bewilderment and is sorry for him ("I see him lookin' […]", p. 55, l. 7ff.). But she knows she has already changed and can no longer go back to what she was before. She realises that Denny is so fixed in his ways and in his thinking that he is incapable of understanding her needs.

Additional information:

The theme of working class individuals trying to break out of a repressive family and community runs through Russell's plays, as is explained in the following quotation:
"[…] the plays are very critical of the tribal, bigoted and conservative elements in Liverpool life because these attitudes can prevent individuality developing. Most of Russell's plays coud be seen as a battle between an individual with a strong sense of his or her own identity, and a working class family or community which represses anyone escaping from the herd."
(J. Gill, *Willy Russell and his Plays*, Birkenhead: Countryvise, 1996, pp. 109–111)

Describe …
The contrast between the way Denny and Frank relate to Rita illustrates the difference between traditional male attitudes to women and the more modern approach which developed as a result of women's emancipation. Denny's expectations of a wife are that her interests should be focussed on her family, that she should have children and provide a good home. His way of dealing with the conflict in his marriage is to grow angry and issue an ultimatum.
Frank, on the other hand, is used to women who know their own mind and make their own decisions. He respects their wishes and does not try to force them to do anything against their will. At various points in the play he expresses his unwillingness to teach Rita, nevertheless, he respects her wishes. He knows that she will accept no one else as a teacher and that if he refuses he will be denying her an education. Against his will, he agrees to transform her.
The movement towards more self-determination for women inevitably had an effect on men's behaviour. Gradually, men realised that they, too, had to change. This affected every aspect of their lives, from helping with household chores and children to the way they treated women. Because women would no longer allow men to dictate to them men had to learn to give them more freedom and room to develop.

IV Rita's Choices

13. List the choices which Rita sees before her at the end of the play. Suggest a few other things she could do. Can you imagine why she does not want to accompany Frank to Australia?

Rita tells Frank that she does not yet know what she will do in the future, "I might go to France. I might go to me mother's. I might even have a baby" (p. 110, ll. 23–24). She may continue with her education and even get a teaching job.
There could be several reasons why Rita does not want to accompany Frank to Australia. One may be that she does not love him and wants to avoid a closer relationship. Or maybe Australia is too far away and she would not see much of her family and friends. The main reason, however, is probably that Rita has only just freed herself from the demands and expectations of other people. After escaping from her restrictive working class environment she became dependent on her teacher. In order to take complete control of her life she now needs to become independent of him, too. She is not yet ready to commit herself to any one course of action. As she herself says, "I'll make a decision. I'll choose" (p. 110, ll. 24–25).

14. Does it matter what Rita decides to do? Do you see any wider social and political implications in the play?

It does not really matter what Rita does. The main thing is that she has begun to realise her potential and has gained enough self-confidence to create a more meaningful life for herself. Her education has enabled her to escape from the constraints of her old life. However, at the end of the play she also recognises the limitations of academic learning. In order to gain real freedom of choice she not only had to open her mind to new knowledge, but also had to learn to think in a new, analytical way. Now she can use these skills to make informed decisions based on critical reflection, not on emotional impulses and traditional behaviour patterns, as before.
The play can be seen as an encouragement to those who would like to make more of their lives. This might not necessarily be through education, but Russell certainly does suggest that a better education can be helpful in widening people's choices in general. When it was written, in 1979, it was almost unheard of for a working class adult, man or woman, to return to education. Since then it has become much more accepted for people to catch up on things they missed at school and there are many institutions to help them. The wider political message of the play has been described as follows:

"*Educating Rita* is an optimistic piece and it is inclusive enough to appeal to wide-ranging audiences. Although it cannot be described as a play that advocates political empowerment, it certainly has the capacity to suggest the importance of education as a tool for working-class emancipation. Furthermore, by creating an accessible play that essentially sees the play from Rita's working-class point of view, it is written to galvanize others to follow her course."
(C. N. Jones, *Populism, the Mainstream Theatre, and the Plays of Willy Russell*, UMI Dissertation Information Services, Ann Arbor, Mich., 1989, p. 245)

Additional information:

Russell himself once explained his own point of view in an interview:
"What the film and play are about is not really somebody who has to be educated but about somebody who had to arrive at a point in her life where she had more control over her life, more choice. She says, 'I don't know how I'll exercise that choice, I might have a baby. I might go back to me mother's, I might go to Australia.' Her actual choice is not important, what decision she comes up with is not important. She tells Frank, 'What's important is you have brought me to this stage in my life where I can have the exercise of choice and I did not have it before'."
(Gill, 1996, p. 41)

Acknowledgements

S. 14: Getty Images, München. Ian Tyas / Keystone Features – S. 22: Aus: Christine Science Monitor 1984 – S. 40: Getty Images, München. Charles Hewitt / Picture Post – S. 58: UNISON advertisement 1994 – S. 61: Corbis, Düsseldorf / Angelo Hornak – S. 79: RED STAR WEEKLY April 1955

Der Verlag hat sich nach bestem Wissen und Gewissen bemüht, alle Inhaber von Urheberrechten an Texten und Abbildungen zu diesem Werk ausfindig zu machen. Sollte das in irgendeinem Fall nicht korrekt geschehen sein, bitten wir um Entschuldigung und bieten an, gegebenenfalls in einer nachfolgenden Auflage einen korrigierten Quellennachweis zu bringen.